THE ULTIMATE
FINAL FANTASY XIV
ONLINE
COOKBOOK

THE ULTIMATE
FINAL FANTASY XIV ® ONLINE
COOKBOOK

The Essential Culinarian
Guide to Hydaelyn

Victoria Rosenthal

INSIGHT
EDITIONS

SAN RAFAEL • LOS ANGELES • LONDON

CONTENTS

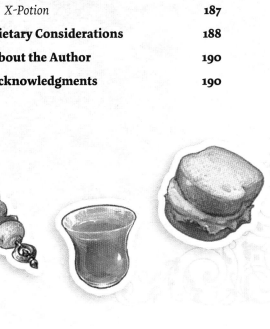

FOREWORD

Thank you for your interest in this book!

Herein you'll find recipes for dishes that appear in the video game FINAL FANTASY XIV.

Our development team goes to great lengths in devising the recipes to be featured in the game, by researching various cuisines across the globe, arranging those to match the world settings in FFXIV, as well as considering what types of ingredients and seasonings would be used for them in-game.

In this book, the recipes of those in-game dishes have been arranged so that they can be reproduced using real-life ingredients and seasonings. It's been a truly interesting endeavor and you'll be sure to savor the delicious flavors in every dish. So, I hope that you, our Warriors of Light, will enjoy trying your hand at "crafting" them.

On a final note, for those of you who may have thought of this as just another cookbook when you picked it up, why not take this opportunity to jump into the world of FFXIV? I'd be very happy if this inspires you to give the game a go!

Naoki Yoshida
FINAL FANTASY XIV PRODUCER & DIRECTOR

本書をお手にとっていただき、ありがとうございます！
この本は、「ファイナルファンタジーXIV」というビデオゲームに登場する料理の
レシピ本です。

開発チームは世界中の料理を研究し、それをFFXIVの世界に合うようにアレンジし、
ゲーム内の料理がどんな素材でできているのか、そして使用する調味料はなんなのか、
そこまで考案してゲーム内レシピを作成しています。

この本ではFFXIVの世界に登場する料理を、今度は現実の素材や調味料で作れるように
アレンジ。 なんとも面白い試みではありますが、どれも美味しくいただける内容に
なっていますので、 光の戦士であるみなさんは、ぜひ、各料理の"製作"に取り組んで
みてください。

最後に、普通の料理本だと思って手に取った方がいらっしゃれば、
どうぞ今度はこの本をきっかけに、FFXIVの世界に遊びにきてみてくださいね！

ファイナルファンタジーXIV　プロデューサー兼ディレクター
吉田 直樹

INTRODUCTION

Welcome, welcome, to my greatest creation yet! This must be the very start of your journey through the wonderful world of cooking—a tasty adventure for all, yes, yes! Ah, but I must introduce myself first. I am Gourmand Gyohan, the soon-to-be famous Namazu Culinarian. Back in Dhoro Iloh, we Namazu are hosting a great festival for all to come and enjoy! You will, yes, yes? Perhaps you'll visit and spend lots of money, yes, yes? You see, this festival is necessary if we are to avoid calamity and save our people. And a festival without the best food around is no festival at all. I decided to become the best cook around and strive for culinary greatness, but out of the blue, I was visited by greatness themselves!

You know the Warrior of Light, yes, yes? I was working on a new cooking collaboration and requested Seigetsu send someone to assist. To my surprise, the Warrior of Light shows up at my campfire, offering a hand! They did what I asked to help me create a great dish of Namazu stylings, and the results were still mediocre—a disappointment. Far less disappointing than all my previous attempts! And the components the Warrior of Light contributed were delicious—inspiring. After they left, I decided that my proud Namazu training would never make me the gourmand I wanted to be, so I departed on the first ship crossing the Ruby Sea. I was seeking the Bismarck, a great restaurant where the Warrior of Light first trained. But the ship I boarded ended up in very cold, freezing Coerthas.

Were you going to introduce your co-writer, kupo? Or am I going to have to save you like I did when you were a frozen fish in the highlands? I am Mogria, a master of meandering. I was part of the Mogmenders, but they're always getting their hands dirty. I'm far too busy seeing all the great sights across Hydaelyn, and none are greater than the places the Warrior of Light has been! I had gotten word that they were seen in Ishgard, so I was on my way when I came across two fish legs sticking out of the snow. I was quite surprised to find a Namazu all the way out here, almost frozen solid, and I took him to Moghome to thaw out. Once Gyohan was warm enough to talk, I learned of his cooking journey and just how bad his sense of direction is, kupo.

Indeed, indeed! I was certain I was heading in the correct direction, but Mogria saved my fins from certain disaster. She's quite talented at getting around, you see. So, I asked if she could take me to the Bismarck to which she replied, "Kupo, kupo! I'm already late for my Warrior of Light visit. Another time, kupo!" I was shocked, floored—what a coincidence that I was seeking the same person!

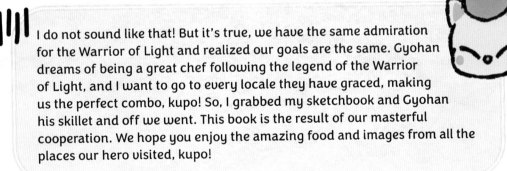

I do not sound like that! But it's true, we have the same admiration for the Warrior of Light and realized our goals are the same. Gyohan dreams of being a great chef following the legend of the Warrior of Light, and I want to go to every locale they have graced, making us the perfect combo, kupo! So, I grabbed my sketchbook and Gyohan his skillet and off we went. This book is the result of our masterful cooperation. We hope you enjoy the amazing food and images from all the places our hero visited, kupo!

Yes, yes, and please visit our festival. ***Wasshoi!***

LOCATION DETAILS

LA NOSCEA

Once Mogria set me in the right direction, I arrived at the epicenter of Eorzean cuisine, Limsa Lominsa, one of the city-states of Eorzea. I learned that all great chefs, the Warrior of Light included, got their start training under head chef Lyngsath Doesfalksyn at the illustrious Bismarck. If I am going to be the best Namazu chef on Hydaelyn, it was only natural that I follow suit, yes, yes! Limsa Lominsa is a port city, making it the perfect crossroads for cuisine of all types and varieties to mingle into beautiful dishes. Because of the major fishing expeditions launched from Limsa Lominsa and its seafaring population, many of these dishes are inspired by the sea itself.

THANALAN

Thanalan does not appear welcoming at first, but the rugged terrain, sprawling deserts, and daunting mountains give way to a unique culture with excellent dishes. The city-state of Ul'dah has wealth and expertise not seen in many other places. Very fancy, very extravagant! And nothing shows that wealth and extravagance better than my favorite theme park, the Manderville Gold Saucer! I have seen, however, that the material wealth doesn't extend to all the many hardworking citizens who work the land to earn a living, making a very interesting contrast in the regional cuisine, yes, yes.

THE BLACK SHROUD

The city-state of Gridania was a great stop on my journey to perfect my culinary techniques. The Botanists' Guild was a wonderful place to learn all about how to better incorporate vegetarian dishes into my repertoire, yes, yes. Compared to the wide expanses of the Azim Steppe back home, the forests of the Black Shroud were nice and comfy. We also got to see some of Mogria's distant cousins, but she was far more interested in sightseeing.

I can see them anytime, kupo!

COERTHAS AND DRAVANIA

Coerthas is home to a great many things: the city-state of Ishgard, the windy peaks of Xelphatol, and copious amounts of rock salt! It was in Coerthas that I first ran into Gyohan and started on our crazy journey. The Warrior of Light spent a lot of time trekking all over Coerthas, giving me lots of neat places to visit, kupo. They even reminded me of all the neighboring areas of Dravania, like Idyllshire and even Moghome...my home!

Mogria, we are supposed to be talking about the food here!

Ah, yes, right, kupo. I love Dravanian kupo nuts; they're so different from the ones found in the Black Shroud, and I always carry some during my travels to remind me of home!

GYR ABANIA

From what I heard on my way to Gyr Abania, the region has had a lot of problems and troubles. I didn't have very many culinary expectations, but I was surprised when I arrived. The Warrior of Light clearly had an impact on the people here, yes, yes, as I saw faces full of optimism and determination. Even more importantly, I found lots of great food! Although the cuisine is less extravagant than other regions, it more than makes up for it with spices and flavors that will impress and astound!

HINGASHI

Because of the bakufu's policies on not permitting outsiders to enter Hingashi, the only part of this region I've visited is the port city of Kugane. But that's okay with me, fine with me indeed, because Kugane is full of cuisine to explore. The street vendors and tea houses have a wide range of unique flavors. The Shiokaze Hostelry is a beautiful tavern with the best sake around, and the architecture is a sight to behold. I wonder if I could get a better view of the rest of Hingashi if I were to have Mogria help me climb to the top?

OTHARD

Othard is the region where I come from. It has so many different groups and cultures living together that it's hard to pin it down, but you can always expect to find something new, yes, yes! Of course, Namazu cooking is superior, but Xaelan, Doman, and Yanxian cuisine all have their own unique flavors. If I were to suggest one place to definitely visit, it would be the festival taking place at Dhoro Iloh! Enjoy your time and spend lots of money. Wasshoi!

NORVRANDT

As a master meanderer, I have been to many areas across Hydaelyn. Most of the time, I'm tracking down the Warrior of Light to see what they are up to. But for a period of time, I wasn't quite sure where they went, and I've since found notes of a place called Norvrandt, kupo. I'm not sure why I've never heard of it before, but the recipes that have come from there seem to have different twists on what I expect or are something entirely new. I'll get there eventually and see what the Warrior of Light was up to, kupo!

INGREDIENTS GUIDE

 Take it from me, there are many ingredients out there to explore. I thought myself a Namazu Culinarian, yes, yes, but I learned just how little I actually knew once I visited places outside Hingashi. I thought to note some less common ingredients here to hopefully help if you too find yourself staring at something you've never heard of before, or maybe when you can't even find it! I just hope Mogria didn't take them all again.

ABURAAGE are thinly sliced, deep-fried tofu pockets used in Japanese cuisine.

BEECH MUSHROOMS are a type of mushroom with a savory, nutty flavor profile used in Asian cuisine. They can be stored in the refrigerator for up to two weeks.

BEET SUGAR is made from sugar beets, a white root vegetable. It can be replaced with white sugar.

BIRCH SYRUP is made from birch sap. It must be stored in the refrigerator after opening. Birch syrup can be replaced with maple syrup.

BLACK VINEGAR is a dark, fermented vinegar made from glutinous rice. It has an acidic yet slightly sweet flavor. If needed, you can substitute another rice vinegar for black vinegar. Black vinegar should be stored in a cool pantry.

BONITO FLAKES, also known as katsuobushi, are dried tuna shavings. They are a key ingredient in Japanese cuisine and one of the major components in dashi. Bonito flakes can be used to enhance the flavors of stocks and used as a garnish. Bonito flakes should be stored in a cool pantry.

DASHI STOCK is a basic fish stock used in Japanese cuisine. It is made by combining kombu and bonito flakes with water. Dashi stock must be stored in the refrigerator once cooked, and it can be stored for up to five days.

FISH SAUCE is a sweet, salty, pungent sauce made from fermented anchovies and salt. The salt content in fish sauce is high—it can be used as a salt substitute to add an extra layer of umami. Be careful to not add too much because it can easily overpower a dish. Fish sauce can be stored in the pantry for two to three years.

FURIKAKE is a dried seasoning used in Japanese cuisine for rice. It typically includes bonito flakes, seaweed, sesame seeds, sugar, and salt. It comes in a lot of different varieties such as wasabi furikake, shiso furikake, and others. Furikake can be stored in the pantry for one year.

GAI LAN, also called Chinese broccoli, is a leafy vegetable with a thick stem.

GLUTINOUS RICE FLOUR is sweet rice ground into flour. Rice flour not labeled as glutinous is made from non-sweet rice. In Japanese cuisine, there are two kinds of glutinous rice flour: mochiko and shiratamako. Mochiko has the consistency of flour, while shiratamako consists of large, coarse granules.

JOSHINKO is short-grain rice ground into a non-glutinous flour. It is primarily used in chewy, sweet dishes.

KIEPOUNDASA is a garlicky, smoked pork sausage that is a staple in Polish cuisine.

KIRIMOCHI is dried, cut mochi pieces. Mochi is a rice cake made from pounding glutinous rice into a paste that is then molded.

KOMBU is a type of dried kelp used in Japanese cuisine. Kombu can be used to enhance the flavors of stocks. It should be stored in a cool pantry.

KONNYAKU is a flavorless, gelatinous food made from konjac, which is a plant in the taro family. Its texture is very chewy and bouncy. It can be stored in the refrigerator in an airtight container.

MISO is a paste made of fermented soybeans used in Japanese cuisine. Miso comes in several varieties including white (the mildest flavor), and red (allowed to age for longer, making it saltier and giving it a stronger flavor). Miso can be stored in an airtight container in the refrigerator.

NIBOSHI is dried young sardines. It can be enjoyed as a snack or used for seasoning stocks.

NISHIME KOMBU is a dried seaweed that is softer than regular kombu.

NORI is a dried edible sheet of seaweed used in Japanese cuisine. It is most commonly used to wrap sushi rolls. Nori can be stored in a cool pantry.

ODEN SET is a package containing fish cakes and fish balls used for oden (a Japanese stew). These sets are perfect to add a nice variety of options in the stew.

THAI BASIL is an herb with purple stems and green leaves used in Southeast Asian cuisine. It has a licorice-like and mildly spicy flavor. It is a slightly sturdier herb than Italian basil and is more stable at higher cooking temperatures. Any type of basil can be substituted for Thai basil, but the results will have a different flavor profile.

TOBIKO is flying fish roe. It can be stored in the refrigerator in an airtight container.

TONKATSU SAUCE is a thick, sweet sauce used in Japanese cuisine. It can be stored in the pantry. Once opened, it can be stored in the refrigerator in an airtight container for about two months.

UNAGI is freshwater eel that is grilled and brushed with a sweet soy sauce. Unagi can be bought precooked and packaged either frozen or refrigerated. If frozen, follow the instructions on the package to heat it up.

WAKAME is a lightly sweet seaweed. It is typically rehydrated when served in dishes. It can be stored in the pantry.

BREAKFAST

ALMOND CREAM CROISSANTS

I sometimes meander to the Jeweled Crozier in Ishgard when I'm bored, kupo. It's got such great views and the honeydew almonds from the markets are almost as good as kupo nuts. I took Gyohan along to show him my favorite spots, but all he cared about were the almonds that he needed to make some breakfast croissants. I guess I should have expected as much; he has such a one-track mind sometimes! I can't imagine being so interested in nuts, kupo.

Difficulty: Easy · **Prep Time:** 1 hour · **Rest Time:** 12 hours · **Cook Time:** 15 minutes
Yield: 6 servings · **Dietary Notes:** Vegetarian

Equipment: Wire rack, medium saucepan, whisk, large bowl, spatula, knife, 9-by-13-inch (23-by-33-cm) baking sheet

6 large croissants

Syrup

2 tablespoons birch syrup
⅓ cup (90 g) granulated sugar
¼ cup (60 ml) amaretto
1 cup (250 ml) water

Almond Filling

1 cup (250 g) unsalted butter
½ cup (100 g) granulated sugar
2 eggs
1 teaspoon vanilla extract
1¼ cups (180 g) almond flour, plus more as needed
1 teaspoon salt

½ cup (60 g) sliced almonds
Powdered sugar

1. Place the croissants on a wire rack and leave uncovered overnight.

2. Preheat oven to 350°F (177°C). Line a baking sheet with parchment paper and set aside until needed.

3. To make the syrup, in a medium saucepan over medium heat, combine all the syrup ingredients. Bring to a light simmer, stirring occasionally, until the sugar dissolves. Set aside to cool.

4. To make the almond filling, in a large bowl, whip the butter and sugar until well combined and fluffy. Add the eggs and vanilla and mix until just combined. Add the almond flour and salt and mix until the mixture thickens. If the mixture appears too thin, add additional almond flour.

5. To assemble, cut each croissant open all the way through. Dip the cut sides of each croissant in the syrup and place on the prepared baking sheet, cut side up. Spread 3 to 4 spoonfuls of the filling on the bottom half of each croissant. Sprinkle sliced almonds over the filling and top with the other half of the croissant. Brush the top of each croissant with additional syrup. Spread the remaining filling on top of each croissant and sprinkle with additional almond slices.

6. Bake until the croissants are golden brown, 15 to 18 minutes. Transfer the croissants to a cooling rack and let cool before dusting them with powdered sugar.

THE MINSTREL'S BALLAD: ALMOND CREAM CROISSANTS

Mogria and I ran into an enigmatic bard in the Rising Stones who overheard us working on our book and asked how it was going. I told him a story of how I took some delicious croissants from the market and turned them into my newest creation, almond croissants. He must have been quite impressed by my feat, yes, yes, or perhaps he was a bit hungry? He broke out into song and performed a beautiful tale of croissant proportions. As the final notes faded, I saw within my mind a croissant primal, layers upon layers 40 malms tall, bearing down on me. A brand new recipe coalesced in my head. What if I made the flaky, buttery, croissants myself? Wasshoi!

Difficulty: Extreme · **Prep Time:** 2 hours · **Rest Time:** 27 hours · **Cook Time:** 20 to 25 minutes
Yield: 6 large croissants · **Dietary Notes:** Vegetarian

Equipment: Small bowl, medium bowl, rolling pin, large chef's knife or pizza cutter, 9-by-13-inch (23-by-33-cm) baking sheet, parchment paper

Phase 1

Butter Block

10 tablespoons (140 g) unsalted butter

1. Prepare a piece of parchment paper by drawing a 4-inch (10 cm) square on the backside of it. Cut the butter into equally thick pieces. Arrange the butter into the square on the parchment paper. Fold the parchment paper over the butter and make sure it is square shaped. Take a rolling pin and smooth the butter into the square shape, merging the butter together into one solid piece. Wrap in plastic wrap and place in the refrigerator for at least 30 minutes to keep cold.

Phase 2

Dough	2 tablespoons (30 g) sugar
3 tablespoons (45 g) water	½ tablespoon (6 g) salt
¼ cup + 2 tablespoons (90 g) whole milk	1 tablespoon (5 g) almond extract
½ tablespoon (6 g) yeast	1½ tablespoons (20 g) unsalted butter, melted
1¾ cups (250 g) bread flour	

2. Heat the water and milk between 100°F (38°C) to 110°F (43°C). Add the yeast and allow to bloom, about three minutes. Combine the bread flour, sugar, and salt in a large bowl. Add the yeast mixture, almond extract, and melted butter.

3. Mix together until it comes together. Transfer to a floured surface and knead until smooth. Place in a bowl, cover, and let rest for ten minutes.

4. Take the rested dough and lightly pull on the edge of the dough to the center and pat down. Repeat this around the entire dough. Flip over (smooth side facing up), cover, and rest for another ten minutes. Once again, pull the edges to the center and pat down again. Flip, cover again, and rest for another twenty-five minutes.

5. Transfer the dough to a sheet of parchment paper and roll out to a rough 7-inch (18-cm) square. Fold the parchment paper over the dough into a 7-inch (18-cm) square. Use a rolling pin to make sure the dough fills the parchment square and is even. Wrap with plastic wrap and place in the refrigerator for 18 to 24 hours.

Phase 3

1 egg

6. The next day, flour a countertop. Remove the dough from the plastic and parchment wrapping and place the dough onto the floured countertop. Lightly flour the top of the dough. With a rolling pin, roll each of the corners.

7. Take the butter block out of its wrappings and place it in the center diagonally. Fold each of the dough corners over the butter like sealing an envelope. Lightly tap with the rolling pin and let rest for three minutes.

8. Flip the dough over so the smooth side is facing upwards. Lightly press down the dough with the rolling pin. Roll out the dough to a 16-inch-long rectangle.

9. Take the bottom of the rectangle and fold it three-fourths of the way up. Take the top of the dough and fold it to have both edges touching one another. Take the new bottom of the rectangle and fold it to the new top. Turn it 90° and lightly tap down with the rolling pin. Wrap in plastic wrap and let rest in the refrigerator for 90 minutes.

10. Remove the dough from the refrigerator, take it out of the plastic wrap, and place on a floured countertop. Make sure the dough is positioned in the long direction, vertically from you. Take a rolling pin and tap down on the dough once more. Roll out the dough to a 16-inch-long rectangle.

11. Take the top of the rectangle and roll it two-thirds of the way down. Fold the bottom edge of the dough up and over. You should end up with a rough square shape at this point. Once again, wrap in plastic wrap and place in the refrigerator to rest for 1 hour.

12. Remove the dough from the refrigerator, take it out of the plastic wrap, and place on a floured countertop. This time, roll the dough to a large rectangle that is ¼ inch (6 mm) thick (should be about 12-by-9 inches (30-by-23 cm) wide).

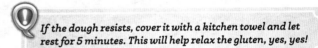

If the dough resists, cover it with a kitchen towel and let rest for 5 minutes. This will help relax the gluten, yes, yes!

13. Cut marks at the bottom and top 4 inches (10 cm) apart from one another. Using either a large chef's knife or a pizza cutter, connect the bottom mark to the top to cut into three rectangles. Cut each of those rectangles diagonally into two large triangles making six pieces in total. Take one of the triangles and tightly roll the widest edge to the thin part, making sure the tip is in the center.

14. On a baking sheet with parchment paper, place the rolled triangle tip-side on the bottom, to prevent it from unrolling when it bakes. Repeat this with the remaining triangles, making sure to give each of the croissants about 3 inches (7½ cm) of space between each other. Cover with a kitchen towel and let rest in a warm spot for 1 hour, or until the croissants have doubled in size.

15. Preheat an oven to 390°F (199°C). Whisk an egg for an egg wash. Carefully brush each of the proofed croissants. Make sure to not apply any pressure that could cause the croissants to deflate. Place the baking sheet in the oven and reduce the heat to 350°F (177°C). Bake for 18 to 25 minutes or until golden brown and cooked through.

Phase 4

16. Follow the steps of Almond Croissants (page 19) using the croissants baked in Phase 3 to complete this trial.

DODO OMELETTE

This Plainsfolk dish took me many tries to learn. A lot of whisking makes my fins hurt. Eventually, the merchant at Reunion stopped selling me dodo eggs—something about wasting food and being ungrateful—so I needed a clever disguise to purchase their wares. I borrowed some pages from Seigetsu's books and made a clever hat, but it did not work, and I had to ask Mogria for help. Also please do not tell Seigetsu; he has many books and will probably not notice, no, no.

Difficulty: Medium · **Prep Time:** 45 minutes · **Rest Time:** 15 minutes
Yield: 2 servings · **Dietary Notes:** Dairy, Vegetarian

Equipment: Small saucepan, whisk, medium frying pan

Sauce
1 tablespoon tonkatsu sauce
1 tablespoon tomato paste
1 tablespoon honey
3 tablespoons (42 g) ketchup
2 tablespoons water

Rice
1 tablespoon butter
¼ onion, diced
3 shiitake mushrooms
2 tablespoons frozen peas
1 cup (200 g) cooked rice
1 tablespoon ketchup
2 teaspoons soy sauce
Salt
Pepper

Per Serving
2 duck eggs
2 tablespoons goat milk
1 teaspoon canola oil

1. Whisk together the ingredients in a small saucepan. Heat over medium-high heat and cook until heated throughout and well combined, about 2 minutes. Set aside until you are ready to serve.

2. Place butter in a medium pan over medium-high heat and allow to melt. Add the onion and mushrooms. Cook until softened, about 5 minutes. Add the frozen peas and cook for another minute. Season generously with salt and pepper.

3. Add the rice, ketchup, and soy sauce to the pan and stir until combined. Season with additional salt and pepper, if needed. Remove from the heat and divide the rice into two portions.

4. In a large bowl, whisk together the eggs and milk. Heat a medium frying pan over medium-high heat. Add the canola oil and allow it to heat up.

5. Add the eggs to the pan and whisk for a couple of seconds. Tilt the pan and cover the bottom with the eggs. Reduce the heat to low and let the bottom of the eggs completely set. The top will be a bit runny.

6. Place one of the rice portions on top of the eggs. Take the edges of the eggs and wrap the sides of the rice. This will not cover the rice completely. Cook until the egg has mostly set.

7. Move the omelette to one side of the pan and carefully flip on to a plate so the eggs are face up and the rice is hidden. Using a paper towel, shape the omelette into a pointed oval. Cover with a generous portion of the sauce.

8. Repeat to make another omelette with the remaining rice.

The duck eggs can be swapped for two large chicken eggs if the merchant gets upset with you!

FARMER'S BREAKFAST

 I was helping open the Bismarck, yes, yes, when someone came into the kitchen complaining about a shipment that never arrived. The head chef figured I hadn't seen enough of La Noscea, so he sent me out to the Red Rooster Stead to pick up some fresh ingredients. When I arrived, some of the farmers were finishing their morning chores and eating breakfast. They invited me to stay for a few bites before I returned to the Bismarck. The dish was simple, very delightful, and a very welcome change from some of the fancier things I had been learning to make.

Difficulty: Easy · **Prep Time:** 30 minutes · **Cook Time:** 45 minutes
Yield: 2 servings · **Dietary Notes:** Dairy-free

Equipment: Medium bowl, 9-by-13-inch (23-by-33-cm) baking sheet, small bowl, whisk, 10-inch (25-cm) cast-iron skillet

Roasted Potatoes
Nonstick cooking spray
2 small russet potatoes (300 g), peeled and cut into large chunks
1 tablespoon olive oil
1 teaspoon salt
1 teaspoon pepper
2 teaspoons oregano

5 eggs
2 kielbasa, cut into large chunks
3 pieces thick bacon, cut into large chunks
2 shallots, cut into large chunks
parsley, chopped

1. Preheat the oven to 425°F (220°C). Spray a baking sheet with nonstick cooking spray.

2. In a large bowl, toss together the potatoes, olive oil, salt, pepper, and oregano until coated. Transfer to the prepared baking sheet.

3. Bake for 20 minutes. Toss and cook for another 10 minutes. Set aside.

4. In a medium bowl, whisk the eggs together.

5. In a 10-inch cast-iron skillet over medium-high heat, cook the kielbasa until lightly browned. Transfer the kielbasa to a plate.
   Add the bacon slices to the pan until cooked through. Transfer the bacon to the same plate as the kielbasa, leaving the grease from the bacon in the pan.

6. Add the shallots and cook until softened, about 3 minutes. Add the roasted potatoes, kielbasa, and bacon to the pan and toss together until well mixed.

7. Pour the egg mixture evenly around the pan, coating the potatoes, kielbasa, and bacon. Reduce the heat to medium-low and cover the pan. Cook until the eggs are just about set, 7 to 10 minutes.

8. Uncover the pan and place under a broiler. Broil until the eggs are fully set. Remove the pan from the broiler and let rest for 2 minutes before cutting into wedges to serve.

LA NOSCEAN TOAST

When I finally arrived at the Bismarck, I found head chef Doesfalksyn and begged him to let me work there. I wanted to train just like the Warrior of Light. He glanced at me and said, "Hah, a fish wantin' to cook o'er dishes? I normally task prospective chefs to make some maple syrup, but let's see ye do the next step first, eh?" and he handed me a skillet and a recipe. This was a simple task, yes, yes, but I still managed to impress the head chef. **Wasshoi!**

Difficulty: Easy · **Prep Time:** 30 minutes · **Rest Time:** 12 hours · **Cook Time:** 15 minutes
Yield: 4 Servings · **Dietary Notes:** Dairy, Vegetarian

Equipment: Serrated knife, whisk, 11-by-7-by-2-inch (28-by-18-by-5-cm) baking pan, 11-inch (28-cm) griddle pan

1 loaf of walnut bread (page 77)
1 cup (250 ml) heavy cream
½ cup (125 ml) coconut milk
5 eggs
2 tablespoons maple cream
¼ cup (60 g) sugar
Pinch of salt
1 tablespoon vanilla extract
1 tablespoon amaretto liqueur
 (optional)
Butter

1. The night before, slice the walnut bread into ½-inch (1½-cm) thick pieces. Let sit out overnight to dry out.

2. The next day, in a large bowl, whisk together the heavy cream, coconut milk, eggs, maple cream, sugar, salt, vanilla, and amaretto. Pour the custard into a deep baking dish.

3. Heat a skillet over medium-high heat. Grease the pan with butter.

4. Place a slice of walnut bread into the egg mixture. Let soak for 30 seconds, turn it over, and let soak for another 30 seconds.

5. Remove the bread from the custard and allow any excess to drip into the dish. Place the bread in the pan and cook until golden brown, 4 to 5 minutes. Turn the bread over and cook the other side until golden brown.

6. Repeat with the remaining slices of bread. Serve with butter and maple syrup.

LEMON WAFFLE

Gyohan was learning how to make waffles, but he felt his recipe was missing something. He asked if I knew where any lemons were, and I said, "Oh yes, kupo! I'll go get them!" There are houses in Mist that have sun lemons growing all over the place, so I grabbed a couple and saved the dish! Maybe I could be a chef too, kupo?

Difficulty: Medium · **Prep Time:** 1 hour · **Cook Time:** 30 minutes
Yield: 8 waffles · **Dietary Notes:** Vegetarian

Equipment: Medium saucepan, whisk, medium bowl, waffle maker

Lemon Curd

3 egg yolks
½ cup (113 g) granulated sugar
1 teaspoon lemon zest
¼ cup (60 ml) lemon juice
pinch of salt
4 tablespoons (56 g) butter
½ vanilla bean, scraped

Waffle

2 cups (300 g) all-purpose flour
1 tablespoon baking powder
1 teaspoon (4 g) salt
3 tablespoons (50 g) beet sugar
1½ tablespoons (3 g) lemon zest
2 eggs
1½ cups (375 ml) oat milk
2 tablespoons lemon juice
4 tablespoons (56 g) butter, melted
   and cooled
½ vanilla bean, scraped

1. In a medium saucepan, whisk the egg yolks, sugar, and lemon zest until the sugar dissolves and smooths. Add the lemon juice and salt. Place over low heat and whisk until it becomes thick, about 10 minutes.

 To test if the curd is thick enough, dip a spoon in the mixture and run a fin or finger across the back of the spoon. If the trail through the curd holds, it is okay! Keep in mind that the curd will thicken as it cools, yes, yes!

2. Add the butter and vanilla bean seeds to the pan. Whisk until the butter is completely melted. Strain the mixture into an airtight container and let cool completely. Place the container in the refrigerator for at least 1 hour before serving. The curd can be refrigerated for up to 1 week.

3. Preheat a waffle maker. In a large bowl, combine the flour, baking powder, salt, sugar, and lemon zest. In a small bowl, whisk together the eggs, oat milk, lemon juice, butter, and vanilla bean seeds until well combined.

4. Pour the wet ingredients into the dry ingredients and whisk until the batter just comes together.

5. Ladle the batter into the waffle maker and cook according to the manufacturer's instructions. Serve warm with the lemon curd.

NUTRIENT-RICH PORRIDGE

We were passing through the Peaks when we stopped at a small mining town called Ala Gannha. I looked around and didn't see anything fancy to eat, but the people were very welcoming and treated us to some nutrient-rich porridge. It's normally a pretty simple fare, yes, yes, but they added lots of spices from the region and made it quite a tasty treat. I just hope they didn't use all their extra spices on us. I need to pay them back!

Difficulty: Easy · **Prep Time:** 30 minutes · **Rest Time:** 12 hours
Yield: 1 Serving · **Dietary Notes:** Dairy, Vegetarian

Equipment: 2 cups (470 ml) airtight container

½ cup (65 g) rolled oats
½ teaspoon ground cardamom
¼ teaspoon allspice
½ teaspoon ground cinnamon
½ teaspoon ginger
1 teaspoon chia seeds
½ teaspoon salt
2 teaspoons flaxseed meal
1½ tablespoons golden raisins
20 grams dried cherries
1 tablespoon beet sugar
¼ cup (60 g) Greek yogurt*
¾ cup (180 ml) milk*

1. Combine the rolled oats, cardamom, allspice, cinnamon, ginger, chia seeds, salt, flaxseed meal, raisins, dried cherries, and beet sugar in an airtight container.

2. In a small bowl, whisk together the yogurt and milk. Pour into the container with the dry ingredients. Close the container and shake well. Place in the refrigerator overnight. Enjoy it the next morning.

* To make this recipe vegan-friendly, simply replace the milk and yogurt with your favorite dairy-free option. I'm a fan of almond milk and coconut yogurt for this recipe!

ORIENTAL BREAKFAST

I heard the Warrior of Light was a big help to the Doman Liberation Front, so I made sure we visited the Doman Enclave on our travels. I thought someone told me it was a disheveled mess, kupo, but the brand-new buildings and shops were a sight to see. We were even greeted warmly by the people there and served a beautiful yet simple breakfast arrangement, kupo.

Difficulty: Medium · **Prep Time:** 1 hour · **Rest Time:** 12 to 24 hours · **Cook Time:** 30 minutes
Yield: 4 portions · **Dietary Notes:** Dairy-free

Equipment: Containers, 9-by-13-inch (23-by-33-cm) baking sheet, medium frying pan, spatula

Pickled Vegetables

¼ cup (60 ml) rice vinegar

½ cup (125 ml) warm water

2 teaspoons sugar

1 teaspoon salt

½ daikon radish, peeled and cut into ½-inch (12 mm) slices

1 cucumber

Salted Salmon

½ pound (227 g) salmon, cut into four portions

1 tablespoon sake

1½ tablespoons salt

Tamagoyaki

4 eggs

1 tablespoon sugar

1 teaspoon soy sauce

2 teaspoons mirin

Pinch of salt

Per Serving

1 salted salmon

3 pieces of tamagoyaki

5 to 8 pieces of pickled vegetables

½ cup cooked rice

1 miso soup (page 89)

1 serving green tea

1. In a large airtight container, combine the rice vinegar, warm water, sugar, salt, daikon radish, and cucumber. If the daikon and cucumber are not submerged, add additional rice vinegar and water. Cover and place in the refrigerator for at least 2 hours. The longer vegetables are left to pickle, the more flavorful they will become. The pickled vegetables can be stored in the refrigerator for up to 2 weeks.

2. Place the salmon in a shallow pan or on a plate and rub the sake over the salmon. Let the salmon rest for 5 minutes. Pat the salmon dry with paper towels and salt the salmon on both sides. Line the bottom of an airtight container with a paper towel. Place the salmon on the paper towel in a single layer. Cover with another paper towel and seal the container. Place in the refrigerator for at least 12 hours and up to 24 hours.

3. Pat the salmon dry and place it on a baking sheet. Place under a broiler and cook for 3 minutes. Turn the salmon over and cook until both sides are crispy, about 3 minutes.

4. In a bowl, whisk together the eggs, sugar, soy sauce, mirin, and salt. Heat a pan over medium-high heat and spray with a nonstick spray. Pour a thin layer of egg into the pan. Tilt the pan and swirl the egg to completely cover the bottom. Let it cook until the bottom of the egg begins to set, 1 to 2 minutes.

5. Fold the outer edges of the egg toward the middle to make a rough rectangle. Take the bottom of the rectangle and roll the egg up away from you until the entire egg is rolled. Place the roll at one end of the pan.

6. Add additional nonstick spray to the pan, move the roll to the opposite side of the pan, and spray the area the roll was sitting on. Pour another thin layer of the egg mixture into the pan. Make sure to get the egg mixture below the roll so that it connects to this new layer. Cook until the bottom sets again. Fold the outer edges toward the middle and roll the egg up. Repeat this process until all the egg mixture is used.

7. Once the egg mixture has been completely cooked and rolled, place it on a sushi mat. Roll the mat up and shape the egg into a log. Hold the egg in this position for at least 5 minutes to let it set. Cut the egg into ¼- to ½-inch-thick pieces. Can be stored in the refrigerator for up to 3 days in an airtight container.

8. Prepare each of the items and serve as a set.

ROYAL EGGS

Sometimes, the fancy people with the big houses in Ishgard make delicious feasts to celebrate special occasions. One time when the Warrior of Light visited, Gyohan wanted me to sneak into the kitchen and take notes on how they were preparing the feast. But I'd much rather be in the festival hall, so I just grabbed the first recipe notes I saw about royal eggs and snuck back, kupo.

Difficulty: Hard · **Prep Time:** 30 minutes · **Cook Time:** 30 minutes
Yield: 2 servings · **Dietary Notes:** None

Equipment: saucepan, heat-safe medium bowl, whisk, 10-inch (25-cm) deep frying pan, 4 small bowls

Hollandaise Sauce

3 egg yolks

1 tablespoon water

1 teaspoon black pepper

Pinch of salt

¼ teaspoon cayenne pepper

8 tablespoons (112 g) unsalted butter, melted

Fresh lemon juice from ½ lemon

4 eggs, each cracked into a small bowl

Water

2 teaspoons vinegar

2 Ishgardian muffins, cut in half and toasted (page 73)

4 pieces of smoked salmon

Dill, for garnish

1. Fill a pot with 1 inch (2.5 cm) of water and set it over medium-high heat. In a bowl that can rest on the pan over (but not touching) the water, combine the egg yolks, water, salt, black pepper, and cayenne pepper. Whisk together for 2 minutes.

2. When the pot of water comes to a low boil, place the bowl above it. Begin to whisk continuously. Occasionally remove the bowl from the heat while maintaining your whisking to keep the temperature from rising too quickly. If the yolks cook too quickly, they will scramble.

3. Slowly add the melted butter to the egg mixture, at most 1 tablespoon at a time. If you add the butter too quickly, the sauce will break and you will have to start again.

A broken sauce means the butter and the egg yolks have separated.

4. Once all the butter has been added, whisk in the lemon juice. Cover, set aside, and keep warm. The sauce will thicken as it cools.

5. To poach the eggs, in a deep, large pan, bring 2 inches (5 cm) of water to a boil. Set a paper towel next to the stove.

6. Whisk the vinegar and a pinch of salt into the water. Slowly pour each egg into the water. Cook the eggs for 3½ minutes. Carefully turn the eggs over and cook for another minute. Using a slotted spoon, remove the eggs and place them on the paper towel to dry.

7. To assemble the royal eggs, place the toasted Ishgardian muffin slices on a plate. Top each with a piece of smoked salmon. Top the salmon with a poached egg. Generously drizzle the hollandaise sauce over each egg, then top with a piece of dill.

If the hollandaise has thickened too much, add a little bit of water to loosen it.

SALMON MUFFINS

I got word that Lord Hien was visiting the Dhoro Iloh festival, and they needed me to return and help with preparations. I couldn't think of a good dish to prepare until I got back to the town and saw that a delicious order of lordly salmon had arrived. Yes, yes, this salmon muffin is fit for a king!

Difficulty: Easy · **Prep Time:** 30 minutes · **Cook Time:** 15 minutes
Yield: 4 sandwiches · **Dietary Notes:** Dairy

Equipment: Small bowl, medium frying pan, spatula, serrated knife

Reunion Cheese Sauce
4 ounces (112 g) ricotta cheese
2 tablespoons lemon juice
2 teaspoons fresh dill, chopped
Salt
Pepper

Sandwich
6 ounces (170 g) spinach
1 teaspoon olive oil
4 Ishgardian muffins (page 73)
1 avocado, skin and pit removed, sliced
4 to 6 ounces smoked salmon

1. In a small bowl, stir together the ricotta cheese, lemon juice, and dill until smooth. Season with salt and pepper to taste. The sauce can be stored in an airtight container in the refrigerator for up to 1 week.

2. In a medium pan over medium-high heat, heat the oil. Add the spinach and cook until just wilted, about 3 minutes. Remove from the heat and set aside.

3. Cut open each of the Ishgardian muffins. Spread a bit of the reunion cheese sauce on each slice.

4. Lay the avocado slices on the four bottom halves of the Ishgardian muffins. Top the avocado with a large piece of smoked salmon. Drizzle additional reunion cheese sauce on top of the salmon.

5. Divide the cooked spinach between the four bottom halves of the muffins. Place the top half of the Ishgardian muffins on top.

WILDWOOD SCRAMBLED EGGS

The Shaded Bower in Gridania has so many tasty ingredients, but it can be hard to find the freshest varieties unless you arrive early in the day! I woke up before the sun rose to find some inspiration at the market, but Mogria was too sleepy to join, yes, yes. I found some great mushrooms and eggs and came back to make her a tasty scrambled egg breakfast. It all looked so good that I almost ate all of it before she got up.

Difficulty: Easy · **Prep Time:** 15 minutes · **Cook Time:** 30 minutes
Yield: 2 servings · **Dietary Notes:** Vegetarian

Equipment: Medium frying pan, small bowl, whisk, spatula

Sautéed Mushrooms

2 tablespoons (28 g) butter

1 tablespoon (15 g) olive oil

8 baby portobello mushrooms, sliced

3 shiitake mushrooms, sliced

1 shallot, thinly sliced

1 tablespoon lemon juice

1 teaspoon pepper

½ teaspoon salt

Scrambled Eggs

4 eggs

2 tablespoons (30 g) sour cream

1 tablespoon (15 g) heavy cream

1 tablespoon butter

1 tablespoon parsley, chopped

¾ cup (85 g) feta cheese

1. Set a medium frying pan over medium-high heat. Add the butter and oil and melt the butter. Add the shallots and cook until softened, about 2 minutes. Add the mushrooms and cook until they have turned golden brown, 10 to 15 minutes.

2. Remove the pan from the heat and season the mushrooms with lemon juice, pepper, and salt.

3. Whisk together the eggs, sour cream, and heavy cream in a medium bowl. Heat a pan with butter over medium heat until butter has melted.

4. Add the egg mixture and whisk vigorously. Stop and let cook for 30 seconds. Continue to whisk together until cooked through. Transfer to two separate plates. Top with sautéed mushrooms, parsley, and feta cheese.

APPETIZERS

CRAB CROQUETTE

Namazu are used to having seafood dishes, but these crab croquettes use a method I learned called deep-frying that is both very tasty and hurts very much, yes, yes. Please be more careful than I was when making these! Also, wait until they cool before eating them. I also made that mistake as well.

Difficulty: Medium · **Prep Time:** 30 minutes · **Cook Time:** 3 minutes per batch
Yield: 13 to 15 croquettes · **Dietary Notes:** N/A

Equipment: Large bowl, baking sheet, small bowl, 10-inch (25-cm) deep pot, slotted spoon, deep-fry thermometer

3 tablespoons (45 g) unsalted butter
½ onion, diced
1 shallot, diced
2 tablespoons all-purpose flour
1 teaspoon garlic powder
1 teaspoon ground fennel
1 teaspoon salt
1 teaspoon pepper
3 to 4 medium (700 g) russet potatoes, peeled, cooked, and mashed
1 pound (500 g) crab meat
6 ounces (175 g) soft tofu
1 cup (140 g) all-purpose flour
3 eggs
2 cups (100 g) panko

1. In a frying pan over medium-high heat, melt the butter. Add the onion and shallots. Cook, stirring occasionally, until translucent, about 5 minutes. Add the flour, garlic powder, fennel, salt, and pepper. Stir until well combined. Remove the pan from the heat and mix in with the mashed potatoes.

2. Line a baking sheet with parchment paper. Add the crabmeat and tofu to the potato mixture until well combined. Using your hands, shape the mixture into round portions, each about the size of a golf ball, and place on the prepared baking sheet. Refrigerate, uncovered, for 1 hour.

3. Set up three stations for breading the croquettes. Place the flour in a bowl to make the first station. The second is a bowl with the lightly beaten eggs. The final station is a plate of panko. Coat each patty in flour, dip the round in the egg, then roll the round in the panko. Place each coated croquette back on the baking sheet. When all the croquettes have been coated, place the baking sheet in the refrigerator until the oil has heated up.

4. In a deep pot, pour the peanut oil to a depth of 2 inches (5 cm). Heat the oil until it registers 375°F (190°C) on a deep-fry thermometer. Using a slotted spoon, carefully place several of the croquettes at a time in the oil. Cook each until golden, 3 to 4 minutes. Transfer the fried round to the paper towel–lined plate and allow the excess oil to drain. Repeat until all the croquettes are cooked.

DEVILED EGGS

Gyohan stopped by the Forgotten Knight in Ishgard when I spotted a familiar face: a tall, silver-haired Au Ra clad in dark, spiky armor. I remember some moogle friends embarrassing him a while back, so I wanted to offer an apology. I ordered some deviled eggs and brought them to his table, but the look he gave me made me too frightened to speak, kupo! I only got a couple words out before I flew right out of there. What a dark, brooding knight!

Difficulty: Easy · **Prep Time:** 10 minutes · **Cook Time:** 20 minutes
Yield: 12 deviled eggs · **Dietary Notes:** Fish

Equipment: Medium pot with lid, medium bowl

6 eggs
3 tablespoons (40 g) mayonnaise
1 tablespoon (20 g) mustard
1 tablespoon (15 g) fish sauce
2 teaspoons lemon juice
1 teaspoon fresh parsley, minced
Salt
Pepper
Paprika
Sardines (optional)

1. Place the eggs in a medium pot and fill with enough water to cover completely. Cover with a lid and set the pot over medium-high heat. Bring to a boil for 7 minutes.

2. Remove the pot from the heat and place under cold running water. Transfer the eggs to the ice bath and let sit for 3 minutes.

3. Carefully peel the shell from the eggs and then cut the eggs in half. Place the egg yolks in a bowl with the mayonnaise, mustard, and fish sauce. Add the lemon juice and fresh parsley. Flavor with salt and pepper to your liking.

4. Fill each of the egg whites with the egg yolk mixture. Garnish with paprika. For an extra fishy kick, top with sardines.

FOREST MIQ'ABOB

I got a chance to meet and say hello to E-Sumi-Yan on our travels through Gridania. I had heard all about him helping the Warrior of Light and the moogles of the Twelveswood and wanted to see him for myself. He was a bit shorter than I expected, kupo! He wasn't very talkative; instead, he seemed content smiling and listening to me ramble about our journey while enjoying a forest miq'abob.

Difficulty: Easy · **Prep Time:** 30 minutes · **Cook Time:** 15 minutes
Yield: 8 skewers · **Dietary Notes:** Vegan

Equipment: Spice grinder, bowl, whisk, grill, skewers

1 tablespoon dried lavender

Leaves from 2 rosemary sprigs, removed from stem

1 tablespoon black peppercorns

½ cup (125 ml) olive oil

2 teaspoons salt

3 tablespoons (45 g) balsamic vinegar

2 tomatoes, quartered

8 shishito peppers

24 white mushrooms

1. In a spice grinder, blend the lavender, rosemary, and peppercorns until the peppercorns are finely ground. In a bowl, stir together the ground spices, oil, salt, and balsamic vinegar. Add the mushrooms to the mixture and marinate for 30 minutes.

2. If you are using wooden skewers, soak them in water for 30 minutes prior to grilling. Preheat the grill. Add a shishito pepper, a mushroom, a quartered tomato, and another mushroom. Repeat until you use all the vegetables.

3. Cook the skewers on the preheated grill, not directly over the hot side of the grill, turning the skewers until the mushrooms are cooked through, 8 to 12 minutes. If you wish to give the skewers more grill marks, place them over the hot side of the grill for a few minutes. Be sure not to overcook the skewers and dry out the mushrooms.

FUTO-MAKI ROLL

Every fish knows that a futo-maki roll bestows good luck and fortune on those who consume it. Because of the doom that Gyoshin foretold, Namazu keep asking me for futo-maki rolls. I am so tired of making them—my fins are sore from rolling. Please consider making these and contributing them to our festival, yes, yes? I would appreciate it!

Difficulty: Hard · **Prep Time:** 1 hour · **Cook Time:** 30 minutes
Yield: 6 rolls · **Dietary Notes:** Dairy-free, Fish

Equipment: Medium bowl, rice cooker, rice paddle, small bowl, whisk, medium frying pan, small saucepan, sushi mat, sharp knife, fine-mesh sieve

Sushi Rice

3 cups (600 g) sushi rice
3 tablespoons (45 ml) rice vinegar
2 tablespoons sugar
½ teaspoon salt

Tamagoyaki

4 eggs
1 tablespoon sugar
1 teaspoon soy sauce
2 teaspoons mirin
Pinch of salt
Nonstick cooking spray

Seasoned Shiitake Mushrooms

10 dried shiitake mushrooms
1½ cups (375 ml) hot water
1 tablespoon granulated sugar
½ tablespoon firmly packed brown sugar
2 tablespoons mirin
1 tablespoon soy sauce

Rolls

1 tamagoyaki
1 piece cooked unagi
6 sheets nori
Cooked sushi rice
1 cucumber, peeled and cut into long strips
Seasoned shiitake mushrooms
5 ounces (155 g) tobiko

1. Put the rice in a bowl, fill the bowl with cold water, and swirl the rice in a circular motion. The water will become opaque, which means the rice still needs more rinsing. Strain the water out and repeat with fresh water until the water stays clear when you swirl the rice.

2. Place the cleaned rice in the rice cooker, add the amount of water needed according to the manufacturer's directions, and cook the rice.

3. When the rice is done cooking, transfer it to a glass or ceramic bowl (don't use a metal bowl).

4. In a small bowl, combine the rice vinegar, sugar, and salt. Add the vinegar mixture to the rice while the rice is still hot. Using a rice paddle, fold the rice vinegar into the rice. Continue to fold and slice the rice with the paddle until it has cooled down. Set aside.

5. In a bowl, whisk together the eggs, sugar, soy sauce, mirin, and salt. Spray a frying pan with a nonstick cooking spray. Set the pan over medium-high heat and pour a thin layer of egg into the pan. Tilt the pan and swirl the egg to completely cover the bottom. Cook until the bottom of the egg mixture begins to set.

6. Fold the outer area of the egg toward the middle to make a rough rectangle. Take the bottom of the rectangle and roll up the egg away from you until the entire egg is rolled. Place the roll at one side of the pan.

7. Add additional nonstick cooking spray to the pan, move the roll to the opposite side of the pan, and spray the area the roll was sitting on. Pour another thin layer of egg in the pan. Be sure to get the egg mixture below the roll to connect to this new layer. Cook until the bottom of the egg mixture begins to set. Fold the outer area toward the middle and roll the egg up, forming another rectangle. Repeat this process until all the egg mixture is used.

Continued on next page

8. Once the egg has been completely rolled, transfer it to a sushi mat. Roll the mat up and shape the egg into a log. Hold the egg in this position for at least 5 minutes to let it set. The rolled egg can be stored in the refrigerator for up to 3 days in an airtight container.

9. Place the dried shiitake mushrooms in a bowl and pour the hot water over them. Let soak for 15 minutes. Remove the mushrooms. Strain the liquid through a fine-mesh sieve into a saucepan to remove any particles from the water. Remove the stems from each of the mushrooms.

10. Add the mushrooms, granulated sugar, brown sugar, mirin, and soy sauce to the saucepan. Set the pan over medium-high heat and bring to a boil. Reduce the heat to medium-low and simmer for 25 to 30 minutes. Strain the mushrooms from the liquid. Squeeze out any excess liquid from the mushrooms, then thinly slice them. The mushrooms can be stored in the refrigerator for up to 3 days in an airtight container.

11. Slice the tamagoyaki and unagi into 6 long strips.

12. Place a sheet of nori on a sushi mat. Wet your hands, and using your fingers, press a thin layer of rice onto the nori, leaving about ½ inch (12 mm) at the top empty.

 It is very important the layer of rice is thin! Add too much and the roll will break.

13. Starting from the bottom of the nori, place the cucumber, tamagoyaki, shiitake mushrooms, unagi, a row of tobiko, and 2 pieces of imitation crab in a single layer. Carefully and tightly roll the sushi together using the sushi mat. Repeat this with the remaining ingredients to make six rolls. Once made, the rolls can be wrapped in plastic wrap and stored in the refrigerator for up to 3 days.

14. Using a sharp knife, cut the rolls in half. In between each cut, wipe the knife clean with a clean, wet kitchen towel. Cut each of the halves into 3 to 4 pieces.

JERKED JHAMMEL

When we were traveling through Gyr Abania, we stopped in Rhalgr's Reach to see the Temple of the Fist and to stock up on supplies. One merchant suggested a tough but easily transportable jerked jhammel. It was a great snack for the road, but Gyohan ate all of his before we stepped outside of the town, then kept pestering me for some of mine, kupo! I told him to go make some himself, so he went off and made an even better version.

Difficulty: Easy · **Prep Time:** 1½ hours · **Rest Time:** 18 to 24 hours · **Cook Time:** 3 to 5 hours
Yield: 2 pounds (1 kg) jerky · **Dietary Notes:** Dairy-free

Equipment: 21-by-15-inch
(53-by-38-cm) baking sheet, wire rack

½ cup (125 ml) soy sauce
3 tablespoons (45 g) chili garlic sauce
⅓ cup (110 g) honey
¼ cup (60 g) firmly packed brown sugar
3 tablespoons (45 ml) Worcestershire sauce
1 tablespoon garlic powder
2 tablespoons oregano
2½ tablespoons ground cumin
2 teaspoons black pepper
1 teaspoon red pepper flakes
2 pounds (1 kg) boneless leg of lamb, thinly sliced

1. In a gallon-size resealable plastic bag, combine the soy sauce, chili garlic sauce, honey, brown sugar, Worcestershire sauce, garlic powder, oregano, cumin, black pepper, and red pepper flakes. Add the lamb slices, seal, and shake the bag until the lamb is completely covered in the marinade. Place in the refrigerator overnight, or for up to 24 hours.

2. Preheat the oven to 175°F (80°C). Line a baking sheet with aluminum foil, place a wire rack on top of the foil, and spray the rack with nonstick cooking spray.

3. Remove the lamb slices from the marinade and pat dry. Place the lamb slices on the wire rack.

4. Cook until the lamb is dry and chewy, 3 to 5 hours. Turn the slices over at least once during the cooking time. Remove from the oven and let cool completely.

5. The jerked jhammel can be stored in an airtight container in the refrigerator for up to 7 days.

MEAT MIQ'ABOB

At the Quicksand in Ul'dah, I saw a brooding Miqo'te seated in the corner. He was probably trying to keep to himself, but his blazing red duelist attire was hard to miss, kupo. I started giggling when I noticed that the rapier on his side resembled the skewers of meat he was eating, but I think that was just a coincidence. Or maybe it wasn't? Ugh, now I don't know, kupo! I should have asked him.

Difficulty: Easy · **Prep Time:** 30 minutes · **Rest Time:** 12 to 8 hours · **Cook Time:** 15 minutes
Yield: 6 skewers · **Dietary Notes:** Dairy-free

Equipment: Spice grinder, large airtight container, whisk, grill, skewers

Duck

1 teaspoon (2 g) Sichuan peppercorns

½ teaspoon (2 g) black peppercorns

½ teaspoon (1 g) coriander seeds

2 tablespoons garlic paste

1 tablespoon ginger paste

½ cup (125 ml) soy sauce

2 tablespoons mirin

2 teaspoons sesame oil

2 tablespoons honey

1½ pounds (680 g) duck breast, cut into large bite-size pieces

2 tomatoes, quartered

6 shishito peppers

Wooden skewers

1. In a spice grinder, blend the Sichuan peppercorns, black peppercorns, and coriander seeds until the peppercorns are finely ground. Transfer to a large airtight container and whisk in the garlic paste, ginger paste, soy sauce, mirin, sesame oil, and honey. For the duck breast, you can leave the skin on, but keep in mind it will be a bit more chewy than without it. Add the duck breast to the marinade and coat. Cover tightly and place in the refrigerator and marinate for at least 2 hours and up to 8 hours.

2. If you are using wooden skewers, soak them in water for 30 minutes prior to grilling.

3. Preheat the grill to 400°F (240°C).

4. Place a piece of duck on a skewer. Add a shishito pepper and another piece of duck. Add a tomato quarter and a final piece of duck. Repeat until you use all the duck and vegetables.

5. Cook the skewers over the hot side of the grill, flipping to crisp all sides, until the duck is crisped, 8 to 10 minutes.

POPOTO SALAD

I thought I could find something useful for Gyohan in the House of Splendors' kitchen in Mor Dhona, so I peeked in to see if anything seemed helpful. Some of the chefs were talking about a stack of new recipes that Tataru had dropped off. I borrowed one and brought it back to Gyohan. He thought it was very out of place that someone put zucchini in this dish, but after trying it, decided whoever had the idea was onto something, kupo.

Difficulty: Easy · **Prep Time:** 30 minutes · **Cook Time:** 45 minutes
Yield: 4 to 6 servings · **Dietary Notes:** Vegetarian

Equipment: 9-by-13-inch (23-by-33-cm) baking sheet, small bowl, large pot, medium bowl, spatula

Roast Zucchini

Nonstick cooking spray

1 zucchini, sliced into thin quarters

1 tablespoon olive oil

Salt

Pepper

Popoto Salad

1 pound (500 g) russet potatoes, peeled and cubed

A generous pinch of salt

1 carrot, julienned

2 hard-boiled eggs, diced

2 scallions, sliced

Roast zucchini

1 tablespoon (15 ml) rice vinegar

¼ cup plus 2 tablespoons Japanese mayonnaise

1 teaspoon olive oil

Salt

Pepper

1. Preheat the oven to 425°F (220°C). Line a baking sheet with aluminum foil, and spray the foil with nonstick cooking spray. In a small bowl, combine the zucchini and oil. Transfer the zucchini to the prepared baking sheet. Bake until the zucchini is tender and golden brown around the edges, about 15 minutes. Turn the zucchini over and bake for another 10 minutes. Set aside to cool completely.

2. Heat a pot with potatoes, salt, and just enough water to cover. Bring to a boil and then reduce the heat and simmer until the potatoes are tender, 15 to 20 minutes. Drain and transfer the potatoes to a medium bowl.

3. Lightly mash the potatoes and let cool.

4. Add the carrot, eggs, scallions, and roasted zucchini to the bowl with the potatoes and mix until well combined.

5. In a small bowl, mix together the vinegar, mayonnaise, and oil. Add the vinegar mixture to the potatoes and mix well. Season with salt and pepper. The popoto salad can be stored in an airtight container in the refrigerator for up to 3 days.

SANDWICH BASKET

I heard gossip among the moogles about a new Scion of the Seventh Dawn, so I just had to see for myself, kupo. I snuck over to Mor Dhona and found a new face in the crowd, a determined Miqo'te with red hair and fierce red eyes. I apparently wasn't the only person there to see him; he was trying to help by attending to different complaints and problems among the locals. He had a big basket of sandwiches that he was giving out, so I helped myself to a couple, kupo. Oh, there's an idea! I'll tell Gyohan to make his own sandwich basket.

Difficulty: Medium · **Prep Time:** 1 hour · **Cook Time:** 30 minutes
Yield: 7 sandwiches · **Dietary Notes:** N/A

Equipment: Medium pot, medium bowl, plastic wrap

Egg Salad Sandwich

6 eggs

¼ cup (60 g) Japanese mayonnaise

3 scallions, white and light green parts thinly sliced

Salt

Pepper

6 slices white bread, crust removed

Lettuce Sandwich

1 avocado, pitted, peeled, and sliced

Salt

2 thick tomato slices

4 slices white bread, crust removed

½ head iceberg lettuce

Mayonnaise

Roast Beef and Horseradish Sandwich

¼ cup (60 g) sour cream

2 tablespoons horseradish

1 tablespoon mayonnaise

½ teaspoon white wine vinegar

Pinch of salt

4 pieces iceberg lettuce

8 slices roast beef

4 slices wheat bread, crust removed

For the egg salad sandwich

1. Place the eggs in a pot and fill with enough water to cover completely. Cover with a lid and place over medium-high heat. Bring to a boil for seven minutes.

2. Once the timer for the eggs has finished, immediately take the pot off the stove and place under cold running water. Move the eggs to a bowl with ice cubes and cold water and let sit for 3 minutes. Carefully peel the shell from the eggs. Chop the eggs finely and place them in a medium bowl. Add the mayonnaise and scallions and mix until combined. Season with salt and pepper.

3. Divide the egg salad equally between three slices of bread. Top each with another piece of white bread. Tightly wrap each sandwich in plastic wrap and place in the refrigerator for one hour. This will make the sandwich easier to cut. To serve, carefully cut the sandwiches in half diagonally.

For the lettuce sandwich

4. In a small bowl, lightly mash the avocado. Season with a pinch of salt. Generously salt the tomato slices on each side. Place the tomato slices on a paper towel and let rest for 5 minutes to remove some of the moisture.

5. Spread the avocado equally in a thick layer on 2 slices of the bread. Place a layer of lettuce on top of the avocado. Top with a tomato slice and more lettuce. On the remaining 2 pieces of bread, generously spread the mayonnaise. Place the bread slices with mayonnaise on top of the lettuce, with the mayonnaise side down.

6. Tightly wrap each sandwich in plastic wrap and place in the refrigerator for one hour, this will make the sandwich easier to cut. Carefully cut the sandwiches in half diagonally.

For the roast beef and horseradish sandwich

7. Combine the sour cream, horseradish, mayonnaise, and white wine vinegar in an airtight container. Season with salt. This sauce can be stored in the refrigerator for up to one week.

8. Take the 4 slices of wheat bread and generously spread a portion of the horseradish sauce on each of them. Split the roast beef and place on top of two slices of wheat bread. Top each with iceberg lettuce and then the remaining pieces of wheat bread, sauce side toward the center of the sandwich.

9. Tightly wrap each sandwich in plastic wrap and place in the refrigerator for one hour, this will make the sandwich easier to cut. To serve, carefully cut the sandwiches in half diagonally.

STEPPE SALAD

I met a very friendly member of the Xaela tribe in Reunion selling the typical fare of the Azim Steppe. I asked for their most interesting dish for research on my cookbook and they suggested this tasty Steppe Salad. I was very surprised they offered their recipe so quickly, but they said they had never met a Namazu so interested in cooking. I hope this book changes this perception of us Namazu, hope so indeed.

Difficulty: Easy · **Prep Time:** 20 minutes · **Cook Time:** 10 minutes
Yield: 4 servings · **Dietary Notes:** N/A

Equipment: 9-by-13-inch (23-by-33-cm) baking sheet, small bowl, large pot, medium bowl, spatula

1 lotus root, peeled and thinly sliced
½ daikon radish, peeled and
 thinly sliced
2 carrots, peeled and thinly sliced
½ bunch of cilantro, chopped
3 scallions, chopped
1 tablespoon sesame seeds

Dressing
⅓ cup (80 ml) lime juice
1 tablespoon lime zest
1 tablespoon fish sauce
¼ cup (60 ml) rice vinegar
2 garlic cloves, minced
1 teaspoon salt
½ teaspoon sugar
1 teaspoon sesame oil

1. Bring a pot of water to a boil. Place the lotus root, daikon radish, and carrots in the boiling water and boil for 2 minutes. Using a slotted spoon, transfer to a wire rack and pat dry with a paper towel.

2. In a large bowl, toss together the vegetables, cilantro, scallions, and sesame seeds.

3. In a medium bowl, whisk together all the ingredients for the dressing. Drizzle the dressing over the vegetables and toss until coated. The dressing can be stored in an airtight container in the refrigerator for up to 3 days.

TUNA MIQ'ABOB

When Gyohan was busy training at the Bismarck, I had a lot of time to float around Limsa Lominsa and look for things to do. I found a large Roegadyn with a pistol and a rusty sword sitting in a corner with a very tasty looking tuna miq'abob. He looked like a pirate with a rough past, kupo, but then again, so does everyone else in this town! But I don't like bothering pirates, so I let him be and took a note for Gyohan for later.

Difficulty: Easy · **Prep Time:** 30 minutes · **Rest Time:** 2 to 4 hours · **Cook Time:** 10 minutes
Yield: 6 skewers · **Dietary Notes:** Dairy-free

Equipment: Airtight container, whisk, grill, skewers

1½ pounds (680 g) ahi tuna, cut into large bite-size pieces

½ cup (120 ml) soy sauce

2 tablespoons honey

1 tablespoon sesame oil

½ tablespoon olive oil

2 teaspoons garlic powder

1 teaspoon ginger powder

2 teaspoons lemon zest, plus 3 to 4 additonal lemons

1 teaspoon fish sauce

1 tablespoon cilantro, chopped

1. Place the tuna, soy sauce, honey, sesame oil, olive oil, garlic powder, ginger powder, lemon zest, fish sauce, and cilantro in a resealable plastic bag. Seal the bag and marinate the tuna in the refrigerator for at least 2 hours and up to 4 hours.

2. If you are using wooden skewers, soak them in water for 30 minutes prior to grilling.

3. Preheat the grill.

4. Place 4 pieces of tuna on a skewer and repeat with the remaining skewers until all tuna is used. Before putting the skewers on the grill, squeeze lemon juice over the tuna.

5. Grill the skewers on the hot side of the grill until the tuna is cooked through, 4 to 8 minutes, turning occasionally to crisp all sides.

BREADS

BACON BREAD

I learned this recipe for bacon bread while training at the Bismarck. But why is it patterned into the shape of wheat? I am still learning new things about cooking every day, yes, yes, but I was certain that bacon was not grown from the ground. I wanted to ask the head chef but the last time I asked a bad question, he made me do all the dishes! I think it's best I take his word for it.

Difficulty: Medium · **Prep Time:** 1 hour · **Rest Time:** 2 hours · **Cook Time:** 30 minutes
Yield: 4 loaves · **Dietary Notes:** Dairy-free

Equipment: Large bowl, medium bowl, large pot, baking dish, parchment paper, kitchen scissors, two 9-by-13-inch (23-by-33-cm) baking sheets, pastry brush, tongs, kitchen thermometer, rolling pin

2¾ cups (430 g) all-purpose flour, plus more as needed

½ cup (75 g) whole-wheat flour

1 teaspoon salt

½ cup (125 ml) oat milk

1 cup (250 ml) water

1 teaspoon active dry yeast

Olive oil, for greasing a bowl

8 slices thin bacon

2 cups (205 g) ground mustard

2 tablespoons unsalted butter, melted

Flaky sea salt

1. In a large bowl, combine the all-purpose flour, whole-wheat flour, and salt. In a large pan, combine the oat milk and water. Set the pan over medium-low heat until the mixture registers 100°F (38°C). Add the yeast and let it bloom, about 5 minutes. Pour the mixture into the bowl with the flour mixture and stir until the dough just comes together.

2. Using your hands, knead the dough for 10 minutes. The dough should be a bit sticky, but if it's too difficult to work with add additional all-purpose flour. Oil a large bowl.

3. Shape the dough into a ball and transfer to the oiled bowl. Cover the bowl with plastic wrap and let the dough rise in a warm spot until doubled in size, 1 to 1½ hours.

4. Turn out onto a floured work surface and lightly knead the dough and split into 4 equal portions. Shape each portion into a ball and cover them with a kitchen towel. Let rest for 20 minutes.

5. Bring a large pot of water to a boil. Line a plate with paper towels. Add the bacon slices to the water and boil for 5 minutes. Using tongs, transfer the bacon to the paper towel–lined plate and completely dry the bacon. Line a baking sheet with parchment paper.

6. Using a rolling pin, roll one of the dough balls out to be a bit longer than a piece of bacon and wide enough for 2½ pieces. Place a generous amount of ground mustard in the center of the rolled-out dough, but leave an empty border all around the edge of about ¼ inch (6 mm). Place 2 slices of bacon on top of the ground mustard, making sure they don't overlap. Tightly roll the dough into a log shape, pinch the ends together, and roll until the dough is smooth. Place the loaves on the prepared baking sheet. Repeat this step with the remaining balls.

7. Cover the loaves with a kitchen towel and let rest until they double in size, about 40 minutes.

8. Place a rack in the lower third of the oven and preheat the oven to 450°F (230°C). Using kitchen scissors, cut each loaf at a 45 degree angle every 2 inches (5 cm), but do not cut all the way through the loaf. After each cut, move the section left or right from the center, alternating the direction after each cut.

9. Sprinkle a little bit of water over each of the loaves. Place a deep baking dish with 1 cup of water on the rack in the lower third of the oven. Place the baking sheet with the bread in the oven on a rack above the baking dish and bake for 10 minutes. Remove the baking sheet from the oven and brush the top of each loaf with the melted butter and sprinkle with flaky sea salt. Return to the oven and bake for another 10 minutes. Reduce the heat to 400°F (200°C) and bake until the bread is golden and cooked through, about 10 minutes longer.

CORNBREAD

The Bismarck is known very far and very wide for its fancy dishes, but it's not the only tasty place to eat in Limsa Lominsa. After working in the kitchens, my fins would be exhausted and I wanted something simpler, yes, yes. The Drowning Wench has many tasty treats, but their cornbread is an extra-special treat. I enjoyed many evenings with my cornbread and a drink while staring at all the people staring at me!

Difficulty: Easy · **Prep Time:** 30 minutes · **Cook Time:** 40 minutes
Yield: 1 loaf · **Dietary Notes:** Vegetarian

Equipment: Small saucepan, 10-inch (25-cm) cast-iron skillet, medium bowl, whisk, spatula

8 tablespoons (125 g) unsalted butter, plus butter for greasing
1 cup (184 g) cornmeal
⅔ cup (97 g) all-purpose flour
⅓ cup (60 g) whole-wheat flour
¼ cup (65 g) firmly packed light brown sugar
1 tablespoon baking powder
2 teaspoons salt
2 tablespoons olive oil
¼ cup (85 g) honey
2 eggs
1¼ cups (310 ml) buttermilk

1. In a small saucepan over medium heat, melt the butter, swirling it around the pan until it becomes golden brown, about 10 minutes. Pour the butter into a cup and let cool.

2. Preheat oven to 425°F (218°C). Grease a cast-iron skillet with butter.

3. In a large bowl, combine the cornmeal, all-purpose flour, whole-wheat flour, light brown sugar, baking powder, and salt.

4. In a small bowl, whisk together the melted butter, oil, honey, eggs, and buttermilk. Pour the melted-butter mixture into the large bowl with the cornmeal mixture. Mix until it is just combined. Pour into the prepared skillet.

5. Bake until the cornbread is golden brown, 20 to 25 minutes.

HONEY MUFFIN

We visited the Gold Saucer and Gyohan wanted to play Doman mahjong. When we arrived at the Wonder Square, they saw that I was a moogle and made us sit at the novice table! They didn't even let us bet with Manderville Gold Saucer points, kupo. Gyohan had already bought a tray of honey muffins, so I suggested we bet with them instead. Some people say Doman mahjong is difficult, but the trick is to bring extra tiles. Gyohan said I cheated, but my tiles were prettier than his and these muffins are delicious, kupo.

Difficulty: Easy · **Prep Time:** 30 minutes · **Cook Time:** 20 minutes
Yield: 12 muffins · **Dietary Notes:** Dairy, Vegetarian

Equipment: 2 small bowls, medium bowl, whisk, standard 12-cup muffin pan

Crumble
¾ cup (90 g) old-fashioned rolled oats
1 tablespoon all-purpose flour
⅓ cup (75 g) firmly packed brown sugar
½ teaspoon ground cardamom
3 tablespoons (45 g) unsalted butter, cubed and cold
1 tablespoon honey

Muffins
2⅓ cups (360 g) all-purpose flour
1 tablespoon baking powder
½ teaspoon salt
¼ cup (50 g) sugar
¼ cup (56 g) unsalted butter, melted and cooled
1 cup (250 ml) oat milk
1 egg
⅔ cup (225 g) honey
1 teaspoon vanilla extract
Nonstick cooking spray

1. Preheat oven to 375°F (190°C). Combine all of the ingredients for the crumble in a small bowl. Cover the bowl with plastic wrap and refrigerate until needed.

2. In another small bowl, combine the flour, baking powder, salt, and sugar. In a medium bowl, whisk together the butter, oat milk, egg, honey, and vanilla.

3. In two batches, add the flour mixture to the butter mixture. Mix together until the batter is smooth. Prepare a muffin tin with nonstick spray. Divide the batter evenly among the muffin cups until they are about three-fourths full. Top each with the crumble mixture. Bake the muffins until golden brown, 18 to 20 minutes.

ISHGARDIAN MUFFIN

You can find these delicious muffins at the Jeweled Crozier in Ishgard, but where is the fun in that? Mashing dough is lots of fun, yes, yes! And things you make yourself always taste better. I've been trying to explain this to Mogria, but she is certain that food tastes better when other people make it. She said food is even better still if you receive it as a gift, but I'm starting to grow suspect of all the gifts that she finds.

Difficulty: Easy · **Prep Time:** 30 minutes · **Rest Time:** 12 to 18 hours · **Cook Time:** 10 minutes per batch
Yield: 10 to 12 muffins · **Dietary Notes:** Dairy, Vegetarian

Equipment: Large bowl, small bowl, 9-by-13-inch (23-by-33-cm) baking sheet, large nonstick pan with lid, kitchen thermometer

2½ cups (390 g) bread flour, plus more as needed

½ cup (75 g) whole-wheat flour

1½ teaspoons salt

1 teaspoon sugar

1 teaspoon active dry yeast

¾ cup (180 ml) oat milk

½ cup (125 ml) water

1 tablespoon butter

Olive oil for greasing

All-purpose flour, for dusting

Cornmeal

1. In a large bowl, combine the bread flour, whole-wheat flour, salt, sugar, and yeast. In a small bowl, combine the oat milk, water, and butter, and heat to melt the butter. Let the mixture cool until it registers 100°F (38°C) to 110°F (43°C) on a kitchen thermometer. Pour the cooled oat milk mixture into the flour mixture and combine until the dough just comes together. It should be a little sticky but manageable. If it is too sticky, add additional bread flour. Form into a round dough. Brush a bowl with oil and place the dough in it. Brush the top of the dough with oil. Cover the bowl with plastic wrap and place in the refrigerator for at least 12 hours or up to 18 hours.

2. Dust a work surface lightly with flour. Remove the dough from the refrigerator and transfer to the floured surface. Punch the dough down and lightly knead for 1 minute. Shape the dough into a ball. Cover it with a kitchen towel and let the dough rest for 1 hour.

3. Spread cornmeal over a baking sheet and set aside. Roll out the dough to about ½ inch (12 mm) thick. Using a 3-inch (7.5-cm) round cookie cutter, cut out as many rounds as possible and transfer them to the prepared baking sheet. You should have 10 to 12 rounds.

4. Cover the baking sheet with a kitchen towel and let the dough rise once more until the rounds have puffed up slightly, about 1 hour.

5. Set a large nonstick pan over medium heat. Place 3 or 4 of the rounds in the pan, about 1 inch (2.5 cm) apart. Cover with a lid and cook until the bottoms of the muffins have turned golden brown, 5 to 6 minutes. Flip the muffins over and cook, uncovered, until the other side turns golden brown, 3 to 4 minutes. Remove the pan from the heat and let cool. Repeat with the remaining rounds. The muffins can be stored in an airtight container at room temperature for about 5 days.

KNIGHT'S BREAD

The people of Ishgard used to ignore me when I'd get close to their city, but there was a nice Elezen with silver hair that I met in Dragonhead once. He wasn't like the other knights and shared what he called Knight's Bread with me, kupo. I wanted to say hello on our trip around Eorzea but I haven't been able to find him yet. I'm sure I'll run into him eventually though; he has to try Gyohan's version of his favorite snack, kupo!

Difficulty: Easy · **Prep Time:** 30 minutes · **Rest Time:** 24 hours · **Cook Time:** 1 hour
Yield: 1 loaf · **Dietary Notes:** Vegetarian

Equipment: Large bowl, small bowl, whisk, kitchen towel, parchment paper, 10-inch (5½ quart) (25-cm) Dutch oven with lid

1 cup (172 g) dark rye flour
2 cups (307 g) all-purpose flour, plus more as needed
2 teaspoons salt
1 tablespoon dried basil
2 teaspoons yeast
1 tablespoon honey
1½ cups (375 ml) warm water
Olive oil, for greasing

1. In a large bowl, stir together the dark rye flour, all-purpose flour, salt, dried basil, and yeast. In a small bowl, whisk together the warm water and honey until the honey dissolves.

2. Pour the water and honey mixture into the flour mixture and mix until the dough just comes together. If the dough is too sticky, add additional all-purpose flour. Lightly knead for 3 minutes.

3. Brush a bowl with oil and place the dough in it. Brush the top of the dough with oil. Cover the bowl and let rise at room temperature for 2 hours. Put the bowl in the refrigerator and let rise for 18 to 24 hours.

4. Remove the dough from the bowl, lightly knead it, and shape it into a ball. Turn the dough out onto a sheet of parchment paper and cover with a kitchen towel for one hour.

5. Preheat the oven to 425°F (220°C). Place an empty Dutch oven with a lid in the oven and heat for 30 minutes.

6. Cut an X across the top of the dough. Transfer the dough, with the parchment paper, to the heated Dutch oven. Cover with the lid and bake for 25 minutes. Remove the lid and bake until the loaf is cooked, another 10 to 20 minutes. Transfer the dough to a wire rack to cool completely before slicing.

WALNUT BREAD

I wanted to say hello to Kan-E-Senna in Gridania since I missed her when she last visited Moghome. I told her it was because I'm rarely home, kupo, but she's very kind and didn't mind at all. Unfortunately, she had no kupo nuts to share, but she did have something close: glorious Gridanian walnuts that she used when showing Gyohan one of her favorite recipes, Walnut Bread!

Difficulty: Medium · **Prep Time:** 45 minutes · **Rest Time:** 3 hours · **Cook Time:** 40 to 55 minutes
Yield: 1 loaf · **Dietary Notes:** Dairy, Vegetarian

Equipment: Small frying pan, food processor, large bowl, whisk, spatula, 8½-by-4½-inch (22-by-11-cm) loaf pan, kitchen thermometer

2 cups (190 g) walnuts
4 cups (600 g) bread flour
1 tablespoon salt
2 tablespoons sugar
1 cup (250 ml) lukewarm water
2¼ teaspoons active dry yeast
¼ cup (85 g) maple cream
¼ cup (60 g) butter, melted and cooled
Olive oil for greasing

1. In a medium pan over medium-high heat, toast the walnuts. Toss them frequently to avoid burning them. Transfer the walnuts to a food processor and blend until finely crumbled. Transfer to a bowl, add the bread flour, salt, and sugar, and stir to combine. Set aside.

2. In a large bowl, combine the water and yeast. Let rest for 5 minutes, allowing the yeast to become active. Whisk in the maple cream and melted butter.

3. Add the flour mixture to the maple cream mixture in two batches, stirring until fully combined after each addition, then knead the dough for 5 minutes.

4. Brush a bowl with oil. Transfer the dough to the oiled bowl, cover, and let rest until doubled in size, 2 hours. This dough takes a little longer to rise because of the weight of the walnuts.

5. Punch the dough down, transfer to a clean surface, and knead slightly. Form the dough into a log shape that will fit into a loaf pan. Grease the loaf pan and place the dough in it. Cover with a kitchen towel and let rise for one hour.

6. Preheat the oven to 350°F (180°C). Bake the loaf until the top has begun to brown, 20 to 25 minutes. Remove the pan from the oven and cover with aluminum foil. This will help prevent the crust from turning too dark or burning.

7. Return the pan to the oven and bake until a kitchen thermometer registers 190°F (87°C) when inserted into the center of the loaf, 20 to 30 minutes. Transfer the loaf to a cooling rack and let cool completely, at least 30 minutes.

SOUPS & STEWS

BOUILLABAISSE

 I followed an excited crowd out to the ferry in Limsa Lominsa to see what all the commotion was about only to find a line of people in fishing gear waiting to set sail. It took a little persuading, but I managed to convince the Roegadyn running things to let me on the boat. It was so much fun setting out on the seas, catching all the fish I could. Yes, yes, I think I fished up a rainbow as well? Or perhaps that was just the thrill of the fishing trip getting the better of me. Either way, Mogria was upset that I had so much fish in my pockets when I got back, so I had to think of a good recipe to use all of my ocean bounty. I figured a nice bouillabaisse would be just the thing!

Difficulty: Easy · **Prep Time:** 30 minutes · **Cook Time:** 45 minutes
Yield: 6 servings · **Dietary Notes:** Shellfish

Equipment: Medium pot, immersion blender

Broth

¼ cup (60 ml) olive oil
1 onion, minced
3 celery stalks, minced
1 leek, white and green parts minced
1 fennel bulb, minced
2 carrots, minced
¾ pound (400 g) tomatoes, diced
5 garlic cloves, minced
Salt
½ teaspoon saffron
Pinch of cayenne pepper
½ teaspoon paprika
1 thyme sprig
1 rosemary sprig
Zest of 1 orange
½ cup (125 ml) dry white wine
4 cups (1 L) fish stock
2 bay leaves
Pepper

Soup

Broth, from above
1 pound (500g) red snapper,
  cut into large chunks
½ pound (250 g) clams
½ pound (250 g) mussels
2 lobster tails, split in half
15 shrimp, shells removed and deveined
8 scallops, cut in half

Crusty Bread

1 baguette, cut into thick slices
3 tablespoons (45 ml) olive oil
Salt

1. In a large pot over medium-high heat, warm the oil. Add the onion, celery, leek, fennel, and carrots, and cook, stirring occasionally, until softened, about 10 minutes. Stir in the tomatoes, garlic, a pinch of salt, the saffron, cayenne pepper, paprika, thyme, rosemary, and orange zest.

2. Add the wine to the pot and cook until it reduces by half. Add the fish stock and bay leaves. Reduce the heat to medium-low, cover, and simmer for 20 minutes.

3. Remove the thyme sprig, rosemary sprig, and bay leaves. Blend the broth with an immersion blender until smooth. Season the broth with salt and pepper.

4. Increase the heat on the broth to medium-high heat. Once heated, add the snapper and cook for 2 minutes.

5. Add the clams and mussels and cook for another 3 minutes. Add the lobster, shrimp, and scallops and cook until the shellfish open and all the fish is cooked, about two minutes.

6. Preheat the oven to 400°F (200°C). Place the baguette slices on a baking sheet and bake for 4 minutes. Turn the slices over and bake for another 4 minutes.

7. Remove the baking sheet from the oven. Brush each slice with oil and sprinkle with salt.

CAWL CENNIN

We had a wonderful stopover in Costa del Sol. I got to sit by the beach and enjoy a nice glass of wine from Wineport across the river. I told Gyohan to relax a bit, kupo, but he started talking to a Roegadyn chef who was behind on her tasks for the Lord of the town. He ended up helping with food preparation and wasted a perfectly good day over a stove. The Cawl Cennin he prepared was pretty tasty, but I didn't tell him I borrowed a bowl.

Difficulty: Easy · **Prep Time:** 30 minutes · **Cook Time:** 45 minutes
Yield: 6 servings · **Dietary Notes:** N/A

Equipment: Large pot, spatula, blender

2 tablespoons butter

1 tablespoon olive oil

2 leeks, white and light green parts only, chopped

½ yellow onion, chopped

1 shallot, chopped

1 celery stalk, chopped

5 garlic cloves, minced

1 teaspoon salt

½ teaspoon pepper

1 teaspoon thyme

1 russet potato, peeled and cubed

3 cups (750 ml) chicken stock*

1 bay leaf

¼ cup (60 ml) heavy cream

Juice of 1 lemon

Crumbled goat cheese (optional)

1. In a large pot over medium-high heat, warm the butter and oil. Once the butter has melted, add the leeks, onion, shallot, and celery. Cook until the vegetables have softened, about 10 minutes. Add the garlic, salt, pepper, and thyme, and cook for another five minutes.

2. Add the potatoes, chicken stock, and bay leaf. Bring to boil and reduce the heat. Simmer until the potatoes have softened, about 20 minutes.

3. Transfer to a blender and blend until smooth. Return to the pot and stir in the heavy cream and lemon juice until heated through. Remove the bay leaf before serving. Serve with crumbled goat cheese.

 You can make this soup vegetarian by replacing the chicken stock with vegetable stock. The locals swear it must be done with chicken stock, but I've enjoyed it both ways.

EXQUISITE BEEF STEW

My cousin works as a delivery moogle, and I told them to keep an eye out for any letters to the Warrior of Light. They got one the other day from some nice-sounding person named Dulia-Chai who lives in some place I've never heard of, kupo. Apparently, there is a new restaurant with an exquisite beef stew that she wants to take the Warrior of Light to! I told Gyohan that if he learned the same recipe, maybe we could also take the Warrior of Light out for dinner. Don't worry, I gave the letter back, kupo.

Difficulty: Easy · **Prep Time:** 1 hour · **Cook Time:** 3½ hours
Yield: 6 servings · **Dietary Notes:** Dairy-free

Equipment: 10-inch (5½ quart) (25 cm) Dutch oven with lid, tongs, spatula

3 pounds (1.5 kg) beef chuck, cut into large pieces
Salt
Pepper
¼ cup (34 g) flour
4 carrots, peeled and cut into 1-inch (2½ cm) thick pieces
1 onion, sliced
7 garlic cloves, thinly sliced
1 tablespoon thyme, chopped
4 cups (950 ml) beef broth
¼ cup (56 g) tomato paste
2 bay leaves
3 (about 500 g) russet potatoes, peeled and cut into large chunks
2 tablespoons cornstarch
2 tablespoons water

1. Generously season the beef chuck with salt and pepper. Put the seasoned beef into a bowl and toss with flour until coated.

2. In a Dutch oven over medium heat, add 1 tablespoon of oil. Add the beef to the Dutch oven in a single layer, but do not overcrowd the pot. Brown all sides of the meat. Remove and transfer to a plate. Add additional oil if needed and repeat until all the beef has been browned.

3. Add another tablespoon of oil to the Dutch oven. Add the carrots and onions and cook until the onions soften, about 5 minutes. Add the garlic and thyme and cook for another 2 minutes.

4. Return the beef to the Dutch oven and stir until well combined with the vegetables. Pour in the beef broth and add the tomato paste. Stir until the tomato paste is incorporated with the rest of the liquid. Add the bay leaves. Bring to a boil. Reduce the heat, cover with a lid, and simmer for 2 hours.

5. Add the potatoes, cover, and cook until the potatoes are tender, about 30 minutes.

6. In a small bowl, combine the cornstarch and water. Remove the bay leaves from the stew and add the cornstarch slurry. Stir until the stew begins to thicken.

LENTILS AND CHESTNUTS

We had a really tasty dish at Bentbranch Meadows called Lentils and Chestnuts. I had never seen chestnuts so large, but the server said it was because the trees in the Black Shroud are very old, and the Guardian Tree is the oldest! I wonder how large I'll get when I get older, kupo? Maybe I'll be as big as Chieftain Moglin, blessed be his pom!

Difficulty: Easy · **Prep Time:** 30 minutes · **Cook Time:** 2 hours
Yield: 6 servings · **Dietary Notes:** Vegan

Equipment: Medium pot, blender

2 tablespoons olive oil
2 leeks, minced
2 carrots, minced
1 celery stalk, minced
1 fennel bulb, minced
2 garlic cloves, minced
1 cup (200 g) red lentils
5 cups (1.25 L) vegetable stock
1 bay leaf
1½ cups (280 g) chestnuts, chopped
Croutons, for garnish

1. In a medium saucepan over medium-high heat, warm the oil. Add the leeks, carrot, celery, fennel, and garlic. Cook, stirring occasionally, until the vegetables have softened, about 10 minutes. Add the lentils, stir to coat, and cook for 2 minutes.

2. Add the vegetable stock and bay leaf. Bring to a boil, then reduce the heat. Simmer until the lentils have softened, about 20 minutes. Add the chestnuts and cook for another 10 minutes.

3. Transfer to a blender and blend until smooth. Top with croutons before serving.

MISO SOUP WITH TOFU

When we visited Kugane, every restaurant and food stall had miso soup. I wanted to eat soup at all of them before deciding on my own miso soup recipe, but Mogria said they all looked similar and her sketches weren't very different. My favorite was a food stall in Kogane Dori. Simple, simple, yet delicate.

Difficulty: Easy · **Prep Time:** 15 minutes · **Cook Time:** 45 minutes
Yield: 4 servings · **Dietary Notes:** Dairy-free

Equipment: Small pot, fine-mesh strainer, ladle

Dashi Stock

1 kombu
4 cups (1 L) water
1 leek, white and light green part only, cut in half
¼ cup (20 g) bonito flakes

Miso Soup

1 tablespoon wakame
4 cups (1 L) dashi stock
8 ounces (225 g) firm tofu, cubed
2 to 3 tablespoons (34 to 51 g) shiro miso
2 scallions, sliced

1. Place the kombu in a pot with the water and set aside for 4 hours.

2. After the kombu has soaked, set the pot with the kombu over medium heat and bring to a boil. Just before the water comes to a boil, remove the kombu.

3. Add the leek and simmer for 30 minutes. Add the bonito flakes and simmer for 15 minutes. Remove the pot from the heat and let it sit for five minutes. Strain through a fine-mesh strainer. Can be stored in an airtight container in the refrigerator for up to five days.

4. Place the wakame in a bowl with hot water and let it rehydrate.

5. In a small pot over medium-high heat, bring the dashi stock to a low simmer.

> **Be sure to not let the dashi stock boil!**
> **Miso will lose its flavor if boiled.**

6. Add the tofu and wakame to the dashi stock and warm, about 3 minutes. Reduce the heat to medium-low. Place 1 tablespoon shiro miso in a ladle and add a small amount of dashi to it to slowly dissolve it in with the stock. Repeat with the remaining miso, tasting in between each addition until the desired flavor balance is achieved.

ODEN

This recipe for oden is a delicious meal that we Namazu learned from the people of Doma. Delicious, delicious! It has many kinds of fish and other Othardian ingredients—perfect for a festival. You can make it too, even if you don't visit our festival at Dhoro Iloh. But why put forth the effort when we can make this for you? But this is a cookbook, so maybe I'm being too pushy, yes, yes.

Difficulty: Medium · **Prep Time:** 1½ hours · **Rest Time:** 3 hours · **Cook Time:** 2 hours
Yield: 6 servings · **Dietary Notes:** Dairy-free

Equipment: Large pot, fine-mesh strainer, toothpicks

Broth

9 cups (2.1 L) water

2 pieces kombu

4 dried shiitake mushrooms

1½ ounces (40 g) niboshi, guts and head removed

¼ cup (20 g) bonito flakes

Seasoning

1 tablespoon soy sauce

2 tablespoons sake

1 tablespoon mirin

1½ teaspoons sugar

Pinch of salt

Soup

½ daikon radish, peeled and cut into chunks

2 cups (500 ml) cloudy rice water

5 ounces (142 g) konnyaku, cut into triangle shapes

3 strips nishime kombu, rehydrated and tied in a knot

1 package of fish cake and fish balls (oden set)

8 aburaage pouches

2 kirimochi, cut into four pieces

6 hard boiled eggs, shells removed

1. In a large pot, combine the water, kombu, shiitake mushrooms, and niboshi. Set aside for 3 hours.

2. Set the pot over medium heat and bring to a boil. Just before the water comes to a boil, remove the kombu. Add the bonito flakes and simmer for 10 minutes. Remove the pot from the heat and let sit for 5 minutes. Strain the liquid through a fine-mesh strainer into a container. The broth can be stored in an airtight container in the refrigerator for up to 5 days.

3. In a large pot, combine the broth with the soy sauce, sake, mirin, and sugar and stir together. Set aside until you are ready to assemble the oden.

4. In a small pot over medium-high heat, bring the daikon and rice water to a boil. Reduce the heat and simmer for 15 minutes. Drain and pat the daikon dry. Set aside.

5. Add the daikon, konnyaku, and nishime kombu to the pot with the seasoned broth. Bring to a boil and reduce the heat, cover, and simmer for 1 hour.

6. Bring a medium pot of water to a boil. Add some of the fish cakes and fish balls from the oden set into the boiling water. Let cook for 30 seconds. Remove and pat completely dry. Set aside.

7. Open each of the aburaage and place a piece of kirimochi inside and seal shut with a toothpick. Set aside.

8. Add the eggs, fish cakes, and fish balls to the broth and simmer for 15 minutes. Add the prepared aburaage and simmer for another 15 minutes. Serve with bowls of rice and remove the toothpicks from the prepared aburaages.

I recommend serving the oden with rice so that you have cloudy rice water available without wasting any food. Just don't forget to save the water you used to clean the rice!

OROBON STEW

We helped the refugees at Little Ala Mhigo by preparing this scrumptious recipe of theirs, Orobon Stew. Mogria saw the eye stalks on the fish that I was preparing and mistook them for whiskers, so I had to give her a brief anatomy lesson. I don't think she listened to a word I said because she started comparing her whiskers to mine, when all I wanted to do was prepare the stew! Also, my whiskers are far better, yes, yes. **They're NOT!**

Difficulty: Medium · **Prep Time:** 45 minutes · **Cook Time:** 45 minutes

Yield: 6 servings · **Dietary Notes:** N/A

Equipment: 10-inch (25 cm) Dutch oven, spatula, medium bowl

Soup

2 tablespoon butter

1 onion, chopped

3 garlic cloves, minced

2 celery ribs, chopped

4 carrots, chopped

1 tablespoon dried sage

1 tablespoon dried thyme

2 teaspoons dried basil

2 chicken breasts, skinless and boneless

4 cups (1 L) chicken broth

1 bay leaf

Salt

Pepper

Dumplings

1½ cups (235 g) all-purpose flour

½ cup (75 g) whole-wheat flour

1 tablespoon baking powder

2 tablespoons chives, minced

1 teaspoon salt

1 teaspoon pepper

¾ cup (180 ml) buttermilk

2 tablespoons butter, melted

1. In a large Dutch oven over medium-high heat, melt the butter. Add the onion and cook, stirring occasionally, until softened, about 5 minutes. Add the garlic, celery, and carrots and cook until softened, about 5 minutes.

2. Add the sage, thyme, and basil and mix well until all the vegetables are covered. Generously season the chicken breast with salt and pepper. Add the chicken breast, chicken broth, and bay leaf to the Dutch oven. Bring to a boil, then reduce the heat and simmer until the chicken breast is cooked, about 25 minutes.

3. While the chicken is cooking, prepare the dumplings. In a large bowl, combine the all-purpose flour, whole-wheat flour, baking powder, chives, salt, pepper, buttermilk, and butter. Mix together until a stiff dough forms. Divide the dough into tablespoon-size portions. Set aside.

4. Remove the chicken breast from the Dutch oven and let cool. Add the dumplings to the Dutch oven, cover, and cook until the dumplings are cooked through, 8 to 10 minutes.

5. Shred the chicken and return it to the Dutch oven. Cook until the chicken has warmed. Remove the bay leaf before serving.

Mogria recommended the chives. They aren't native to Thanalan but they really made this dish pop.

SKYBUILDERS' STEW

I may be a moogle, but I'm not very good at mending things. The nice people at the Firmament saw me wander in with Gyohan and asked if I could help with the repairs, but I'm pretty hopeless when it comes to that stuff. They asked if I could at least serve soup for the workers, but I'm not sure I did such a good job with that either, kupo. But everyone left with a smile and the soup is quite tasty, so enjoy!

Difficulty: Easy · **Prep Time:** 30 minutes · **Cook Time:** 30 minutes
Yield: 6 servings · **Dietary Notes:** Dairy

Equipment: Large pot with a lid, spatula, medium saucepan, whisk

1 pound (500 g) chicken thighs, cut into bite-size pieces

Salt

Pepper

Olive oil

½ (183 g) onion, cut into bite-size pieces

3 garlic cloves, minced

1 medium (200 g) russet potato, cut into bite-size pieces

1 small (75 g) carrot, cut into bite-size pieces

1 small (135 g) daikon radish, cut into bite-size pieces

2 to 3 cups (500 to 750ml) chicken stock

1 bay leaf

½ cup (85 g) broccoli

Cream Base

3 tablespoons (45 g) butter

2½ tablespoons (35 g) cream cheese

¼ cup (45 g) flour

1 cup (250 ml) milk

1. Generously season the chicken with salt and pepper and set aside. In a large pot over medium-high heat, add the oil, onion, and garlic. Cook, stirring occasionally, until the onion is translucent, about 5 minutes.

2. Add the chicken and cook until it is no longer pink, 5 to 7 minutes. Add the potatoes, carrot, and daikon.

3. Pour just enough chicken stock to barely cover everything. Add the bay leaf. Bring the stock to a boil and then reduce the heat to medium-low. Cover and simmer for 20 minutes.

4. While the stock is simmering, make the cream base. In a medium saucepan, melt butter and cream cheese. Slowly whisk in the flour. Cook until the mixture thickens and begins to smell like bread, about 3 minutes.

5. Slowly add the milk while continuously whisking until the mixture has warmed up and thickened. Remove from the heat and set aside.

6. Add the broccoli to the chicken and vegetables and raise the heat to medium-high. Bring to a boil and cook until the broccoli has softened slightly, 3 to 5 minutes. Pour in the cream mixture and stir until incorporated. Season with additional salt and pepper. Remove bay leaf before serving.

MAIN DISHES

BANH XEO

We ran into an emissary of Nagxia at the Doman Enclave where he was directing some restoration work. Since he was there assisting with the melding together of cultures under Doma, he was instructing the staff on how to prepare a few iconic Nagxian dishes. He spoke with Gyohan for a bit, but I was just admiring the beautiful silks he was wearing. I almost missed making sketches of the dish before everyone ate it up, kupo.

Difficulty: Medium · **Prep Time:** 1 hour · **Rest Time:** 1 hour · **Cook Time:** 30 minutes
Yield: 8 servings · **Dietary Notes:** Dairy-free

Equipment: Medium bowl, whisk, 10-inch (25-cm) frying pan with lid, spatula

Nước chấm

⅓ cup (80 ml) water
¼ cup (50 g) sugar
¼ cup (60 ml) fish sauce
3 tablespoons (45 ml) lime juice
1 Thai chili, sliced
5 garlic cloves, minced

Batter

1½ cups (210 g) rice flour
2 tablespoons cornstarch
1 teaspoon turmeric
½ teaspoon fennel, ground
½ teaspoon cumin seeds
½ teaspoon salt
3 scallions, finely chopped
1½ cups (375 ml) coconut milk
1½ cups (375 ml) water

Filling

½ pound (500 g) shrimp, peeled, deveined, and sliced in half
½ pound bacon (500 g), cut into large chunks
½ onion, sliced
½ carrot, peeled and julienned
½ cup (50 g) bean sprouts, plus a handful more
Mint
Cilantro
Canola Oil

For serving

Thai basil
Bean sprouts
Lettuce
Rice paper

1. In a bowl, whisk all the ingredients together until the sugar has dissolved. The nước chấm can be stored in an airtight container in the refrigerator for up to two weeks.

2. To make the batter, in a large bowl, whisk together all the batter ingredients until smooth. Set aside and let rest for 1 hour. The batter can be stored in an airtight container in a refrigerator for up to 5 days.

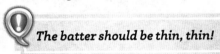

The batter should be thin, thin!

3. Divide the filling ingredients, except for the oil, into 8 equal portions.

4. In a frying pan over medium-high heat, warm 1 teaspoon of canola oil, swirling the pan to coat the bottom. Add 1 portion each of the shrimp and bacon to the pan. Cook for 1 minute and turn them over. Add 1 portion each of the onion and carrots.

5. Pour about ½ cup of batter into the pan. Quickly tilt the pan to coat the bottom of the pan. Top with one portion of the bean sprouts and cover with a lid. Cook for 2 to 3 minutes. Remove from the heat and top with 1 portion each of the mint, cilantro, and basil. Add additional bean sprouts. Fold the pancake in half and transfer to a plate. Serve with the nước chấm, Thai basil, bean sprouts, lettuce, and rice paper.

6. Repeat steps 3 and 4 with the remaining portions. The pancakes are best enjoyed the same day.

BATTERED FISH

This is a very different way to prepare fish than I am used to. The Bismarck serves this fish deep-fried, golden, and truly delicious. If I've learned anything from my time in Limsa Lominsa, it's just how many ways there are to prepare fish that I didn't know about beforehand. Yes, yes, this trip was worthwhile for this recipe alone.

Difficulty: Medium · **Prep Time:** 1 hour · **Cook Time:** 30 minutes
Yield: 6 to 8 · **Dietary Notes:** Dairy-free

Equipment: Large bowl, medium bowl, whisk, 10-inch (25-cm) deep pot, tongs, deep-fry thermometer

Fries

About 6 medium (1.2 kg) russet potatoes, peeled and cut into thick slices

Peanut oil

1 tablespoon turmeric

2 teaspoons garlic powder

¼ teaspoon cayenne

1 tablespoon salt

½ teaspoon pepper

Fish

Peanut oil

1¾ cups (280 g) all-purpose flour, plus flour for coating the fish

1 teaspoon garlic powder

½ teaspoon turmeric

½ teaspoon cumin

½ teaspoon cayenne pepper

12 ounces (375 ml) amber ale

Juice of 1 lemon

2 pounds (1 kg) haddock, cod, or halibut, cut into 8 large pieces

Salt

Pepper

1. Place the sliced potato pieces in a bowl of cold water. Soak for 30 minutes and leave them in the water until ready to fry.

2. Pour the peanut oil into a deep pot to a depth of 2 inches (5 cm). Set the pot over medium-high heat and heat until the oil temperature registers 300°F (149°C) on a deep-fry thermometer. Remove the potatoes from the water and dry well. Begin deep frying the potatoes in batches until soft but not browned, about 5 minutes.

3. Transfer the potatoes to a wire rack and let the excess oil drain onto paper towels or a rimmed backing sheet. Repeat until all the potatoes have been fried. Raise the heat and reheat the oil until it registers 375°F (190°C) on a deep-fry thermometer.

4. Fry the potatoes again until they become golden brown, about 2 minutes. Transfer the potatoes back to a bowl and generously season with the spice mix. Repeat with the remaining fries.

5. Pour the peanut oil into a deep pot to a depth of 2 inches (5 cm). Set the pot over medium heat and heat until the oil temperature registers 300°F (149°C) on a deep-fry thermometer.

 You can use the same oil you used for the fries. I like to fry the fish in between the double fry of the fries, yes, yes!

6. In a medium bowl, whisk together the all-purpose flour, garlic powder, turmeric, cumin, cayenne, amber ale, and lemon juice. If the batter is too thick, add water to loosen it.

7. Season each piece of fish with salt and pepper. Cover each fillet in flour. Set aside until you are ready to start deep frying.

8. Once the oil reaches the right temperature, dunk each of the fillets in the batter, coating them completely. Place the fillet in the oil and cook until the batter is golden brown, 4 to 6 minutes. Flip the fish about halfway through the cooking process to get both sides nice and golden. Serve with the fries.

BOSCAIOLA

I purchase mushrooms quite often at the market, but I thought it high time to get my fins dirty and forage for some myself. I sought out the Botanists' Guild in Gridania and, after a bit of confusion about why a catfish was asking for help, they took me out to the Black Shroud and showed me how to identify and gather mushrooms on my own. This pasta dish is no doubt better with freshly sourced mushrooms. Very delectable, very earthy.

Difficulty: Easy · **Prep Time:** 30 minutes · **Cook Time:** 45 minutes
Yield: 4 servings · **Dietary Notes:** N/A

Equipment: Small bowl, large pot

1 ounce (30 g) dried porcini
  mushrooms

5 pieces bacon, sliced

2 shallots, sliced

5 garlic cloves, minced

1 king oyster mushroom, sliced

4 shiitake mushrooms, stems
  removed and sliced

8 cremini mushrooms, stems
  removed and sliced

1 teaspoon (1 g) fresh thyme, chopped

½ teaspoon (½ g) fresh rosemary,
  chopped

28 ounces (793 g) whole tomatoes,
  crushed by hand

⅓ cup (80 ml) heavy cream

¼ cup (20 g) Parmesan cheese, grated

1 pound (453 g) spaghetti, cooked
    al dente according to the
    manufacturer's directions and 1 cup
    of cooking water reserved

Olive oil

1. Place the porcini mushrooms in a bowl and cover with hot water. Let rest for 10 minutes to rehydrate. Strain and squeeze out any extra liquid from the mushrooms. Chop roughly and set aside.

2. In a large pot over medium-high heat, fry the bacon until crispy, about 5 minutes. Remove the bacon from the pan and place on a plate. Add the shallot and garlic to the pot and cook until softened, about 2 minutes.

3. Add the mushrooms and cook until browned, about 10 minutes.

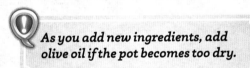

As you add new ingredients, add olive oil if the pot becomes too dry.

4. Add the thyme, rosemary, and bacon. Stir until well combined. Add the crushed tomatoes and ¼ cup of the reserved pasta water. Simmer for 10 minutes. Add the heavy cream and Parmesan. Add more pasta water in small amounts to thin the sauce slightly. Add the cooked spaghetti and serve immediately.

CREAMY SALMON PASTA

I am used to cooking with many kinds of fish, but I have rarely been honored to work with the king salmon. You see, it is bigger than most salmon, but very scarce. Very elusive. I usually have to go to the market and pay a pretty gil for the smoked salmon they have there, but one day I will make this recipe with the freshest ingredients around. Yes, yes, indeed.

Difficulty: Easy · **Prep Time:** 30 minutes · **Cook Time:** 30 minutes
Yield: 4 servings · **Dietary Notes:** N/A

Equipment: Large frying pan, spatula, whisk

¼ cup (50 g) butter
2 tablespoons olive oil
5 cloves of garlic, finely chopped
1 lemongrass stalk
2 tablespoons flour
2 cups (500 ml) heavy cream
1 tablespoon lemon juice
2 teaspoons lemon zest
1 teaspoon fish sauce
1 teaspoon pepper
1 teaspoon dried thyme
1 teaspoon dried oregano
½ cup (60 g) grated Parmesan cheese
1 pound (500 g) gai lan, stems removed and leaves chopped
1 pound (453 g) spaghetti, cooked al dente according to the manufacturer's directions and 1 cup of cooking water reserved
1 pound (500 g) smoked salmon

1. In a frying pan over medium-high heat, melt the butter with the oil. Once the butter melts, add the garlic and lemongrass. Cook until the garlic just starts to brown, about 3 minutes. Whisk in the flour and cook until it blends in with the butter and oil.

2. Slowly whisk in the heavy cream, lemon juice, lemon zest, and fish sauce and bring to a simmer. Cook for about 3 minutes.

3. Add the pepper, thyme, and oregano and whisk together. Add the Parmesan and whisk together until well combined. Add the gai lan leaves and cook until wilted.

4. Add the cooked pasta and mix together. If the sauce is too thick, add a little bit of pasta water to loosen it. Turn off the heat, add the smoked salmon, and stir together until well-combined. Serve immediately.

DEEP-FRIED OKEANIS

I don't understand why the Warrior of Light meets with Aymeric so often. Ugh, just the other day, they were celebrating with a sumptuous meal with a big deep-fried okeanis as the centerpiece. Why do they spend so much time together when it should be ME who spends time with them, kupo! Gyohan wanted me to talk about this dish, but I'm too upset. If you make this dish, please don't invite the Warrior of Light over.

Difficulty: Medium · **Prep Time:** 1 hour · **Cook Time:** 45 minutes
Yield: 4 servings · **Dietary Notes:** Pork

Equipment: Large pot, medium bowl, 9-by-13-inch (23-by-33-cm) baking sheet, 2 large plates, small bowl, 10-inch (25-cm) deep pan, deep-fry thermometer

Potatoes

2 pounds (1 kg) red potatoes, peeled and cut into large chunks

2 tablespoons olive oil

1 teaspoon rosemary

1 teaspoon oregano

1½ teaspoons (4 g) garlic powder

1 teaspoon (4 g) onion powder

Salt

Pepper

½ cup (75 g) all-purpose flour

¼ teaspoon garlic powder

2 eggs

1 tablespoon fish sauce

2 cups (80 g) panko

4 pieces of boneless pork chop, each ¼ pound (125 g)

Salt

Pepper

Peanut oil

1 lemon, cut into slices

1. Preheat the oven to 425°F (220°C). Bring a large pot of water to a boil and add the potatoes. Boil for 8 minutes. In a bowl, combine the oil, rosemary, oregano, garlic powder, and onion powder.

2. Add the potatoes in the bowl and toss with the seasoned oil. Transfer the potatoes to a baking sheet and season with salt and pepper. Bake the potatoes for 20 minutes, toss the potatoes, and then bake for another 15 minutes. Keep warm until you are ready to serve.

3. Set up three stations to bread the pork. On the first plate, combine flour and garlic powder. In a bowl, mix the eggs and fish sauce. On another plate, spread the panko.

4. Prepare the pork by flattening it with a meat mallet, heavy pan, or rolling pin, to ¼-inch (6-mm) thick. Generously season both sides with salt and pepper.

5. Coat the pork in the flour mixture first, coating both sides. Next, dip the pork in the egg mixture, letting the excess drip back into the bowl. Finally, dredge the pork in the panko, turning it to coat well.

6. Line a plate with paper towels and set it by the stovetop. In a deep pan, pour the peanut oil to a depth of ½ inch (12 mm). Heat the oil until it registers 325°F (165°C) on a deep-fry thermometer. Carefully add the pork to the oil and fry until the pork is golden brown and cooked through about 2 minutes on each side. Transfer to the paper towel–lined plate to dry. Serve with a slice of lemon and the roasted potatoes.

MOLE LOAF

We knew that Camp Drybone, and the Church of Saint Adama Landama, were not going to be cheerful stops on our trip, but we thought it was important to follow the Warrior of Light and pay our respects to those we've lost. Gyohan wanted to bring some joy for those going to mourn so he spoke with the locals, stopped by the market, and whipped up this simple comfort food dish.

Difficulty: Medium · **Prep Time:** 30 minutes · **Cook Time:** 10 minutes
Yield: 5 servings · **Dietary Notes:** N/A

Equipment: Small pan, medium bowl, large pan with a lid, spatula

Patties

Olive oil

1 onion, diced

1 pound (500 g) ground lamb

4 garlic cloves, minced

1 teaspoon salt

Pepper

⅓ cup (60 g) panko, plus more
    as needed

1 egg

1 teaspoon soy sauce

1 teaspoon fish sauce

1 tablespoon ketchup

2 teaspoons tonkatsu

Sauce

¼ cup (80 g) ketchup

¼ cup (72 g) tonkatsu

2 tablespoons sake

2 tablespoons water

1. In a small pan over medium-high heat, add 1 teaspoon of oil and onions. Cook the onions, stirring occasionally, until browned, about 10 minutes. Remove the pan from the heat, transfer the onions to a medium bowl, and let to cool.

2. Add the lamb, garlic, salt, pepper to taste, and panko to the onions. In a small bowl, combine the egg, soy sauce, fish sauce, ketchup, and tonkatsu. Add the egg mixture to the lamb and use your hands to mix until fully incorporated. The mixture should be sticky and moist; if it is too difficult to handle, add additional panko. Shape the mixture into 5 patties.

3. In a large pan over medium heat, warm 1 tablespoon of oil. Carefully place the patties in the pan. Cook until the bottom has browned, 3 to 4 minutes. Turn the patties over and cook until the other side is browned, about 3 minutes.

4. Add ¼ cup of water to the pan and cover. Cook until the water has evaporated or until the patties are cooked through.

5. Remove the patties from the pan and set them on a plate. Keep the heat at medium. Combine all the sauce ingredients and 2 tablespoons water in the pan and cook until the sauce thickens slightly, about 3 minutes. Serve each patty with a generous serving of sauce on top.

PAN-FRIED MAHI-MAHI

Some folks from the Fishermen's Guild brought a delivery over to the Bismarck and mistook me for a fresh catch of the day! Very rude, very disagreeable, has no one in this town seen a Namazu before? They didn't believe a fish like me could cook another fish, so I showed them with this new recipe on the menu, a pan-fried mahi-mahi. Yes, yes, they were quite impressed. Maybe next time, they won't judge a chef by their fins!

Difficulty: Easy · **Prep Time:** 30 minutes · **Cook Time:** 15 minutes
Yield: 4 servings · **Dietary Notes:** N/A

Equipment: Medium pan, kitchen thermometer

4 mahi-mahi fillets, skin on
Salt
Pepper
Zest of 1 lemon
2 tablespoons olive oil
2 tablespoons butter
4 garlic cloves, minced
2 tablespoons flour
¼ cup (60 ml) vegetable broth
1 tablespoon sake
Juice of 1 lemon
½ lemon, sliced

1. Generously season the mahi-mahi with salt, pepper, and lemon zest. Heat a pan with olive oil over medium-high heat. Add the mahi-mahi, skin side down, to the pan. Cook the bottom side until crisped up, about 4 minutes. Turn the mahi-mahi over and cook until the temperature registers 137°F (58°C) on a kitchen thermometer, another 2 to 4 minutes. Transfer the mahi-mahi to a plate.

2. In the same pan, add the butter and allow it to melt. Add the garlic and cook until fragrant, about two minutes. Add the flour and mix until well combined. Pour in the vegetable broth, sake, and lemon juice and whisk together until thickened. Add the lemon slices and allow to heat up.

3. To serve, top each of the mahi-mahi filets with a bit of the sauce and lemon slices.

PIZZA

Gyohan sent me to find more food inspiration, but I came across my favorite Scion duo: Alphinaud and Alisaie! They had these weird pie slices with what looked like cheese and some red stuff that I had never seen before, so I took some to bring back. It looked delicious, so I knew Gyohan would be excited to try it, kupo! As I floated away, I heard an argument start to break out. Something about slices and stealing? Those two always find something to disagree about.

Difficulty: Medium · **Prep Time:** 45 minutes · **Rest Time:** 24 to 48 hours · **Cook Time:** 1 hour
Yield: 2 to 3 pizzas · **Dietary Notes:** Vegetarian

Equipment: Medium bowl, large bowl, stand mixer, two or three 10-inch (25-cm) cast-iron skillets, medium saucepan, spatula, basting brush

Pizza Dough

2½ cups plus 4 teaspoons (400 g) bread flour
1¾ teaspoons active dry yeast
2 teaspoons sugar
1 teaspoon salt
1 teaspoon ginger powder
½ teaspoon onion powder
1¼ cups (270 g) water
2 tablespoons olive oil
All-purpose flour, for dusting
Nonstick cooking spray

Pizza Sauce

½ tablespoon olive oil
½ tablespoon butter
3 garlic cloves, minced
One 14-ounce (397 g) can whole San Marzano tomatoes
1 tablespoon dried oregano
Pinch of red pepper flakes
½ teaspoon onion powder
½ teaspoon sugar
Salt
Pepper

To make the pizzas

All-purpose flour, for dusting
Pizza dough
Olive oil
Garlic powder
Onion powder
Pizza sauce
10 ounces (315 g) fresh mozzarella, sliced
About ½ cup (60 grams) grated Parmesan cheese, or more to taste
8 to 12 fresh basil leaves

1. The day before you plan to make the pizza, prepare the dough. In the bowl of a stand mixer, stir together the flour, yeast, sugar, salt, ginger powder, and onion powder. In a small bowl, combine the oil and 1¼ cups (310 ml) water. Pour the oil and water mixture into the bowl of the stand mixer.

2. Fit the stand mixer with the dough hook and mix on low until all the ingredients come together. When the dough has formed a ball, increase the speed of the mixer to medium and knead the dough for 5 minutes.

3. Lightly dust a work surface with flour. Turn the dough out onto the floured surface. Using your hands, smooth the dough into a ball. Spray a large bowl with nonstick cooking spray. Place the dough in the bowl. Cover the bowl with plastic wrap and refrigerate for 24 to 48 hours.

4. Remove the dough from the refrigerator at least 30 minutes before you start to prepare your pizza. Lightly dust a work surface with flour. Punch the dough down and turn it out onto the floured surface. Divide the dough into 2 to 3 portions and shape each portion into a ball. Cover the balls with a kitchen towel and let them rest for 30 minutes.

 If you split the dough into two portions, the crust will be very thick, while in three portions it will be thinner. Either version is delicious, yes, yes!

5. In a saucepan over medium-high heat, warm the oil and butter. Add the garlic and cook until the garlic is golden brown, 2 to 3 minutes. Add the tomatoes and stir together well.

6. Add the oregano, red pepper flakes, onion powder, and sugar. Reduce the heat to medium-low and simmer, stirring often and lightly mashing the tomatoes, until thickened, about 45 minutes. The tomatoes should be well mashed by the end of the cooking time. Taste and season with salt and pepper.

Continued on next page

7. Preheat the oven to 475°F (245°C). Lightly dust a work surface with flour. Pound one ball of dough into a disk shape. Stretch the dough into a disk slightly wider than the skillet. Oil the bottom and inner sides of the skillet (or two or three skillets, depending on how many you are using). Sprinkle a generous amount of garlic powder and onion powder in the skillet. Transfer the dough to the skillet. Repeat with the remaining balls of dough.

8. Spread the pizza sauce evenly over each of the disks. Add several pieces of mozzarella to each, evenly distributed over the sauce. Brush the edges of the crusts with oil. Place the skillet over medium-high heat. Cook until the bottom of the dough begins to turn brown, about 5 minutes. Repeat with the remaining skillets.

9. Transfer the skillet(s) to the oven and cook until the cheese melts and the crust is lightly browned, 10 to 12 minutes.

Fresh mozzarella is high in moisture! Very juicy, very delicious. You might want to dab the pizza with a paper towel to remove excess liquid as the pizza cooks. You can swap out the fresh mozzarella for shredded mozzarella if you prefer.

10. Sprinkle Parmesan over top of each of the pizzas and return to the oven. Cook until the cheese has melted, 2 to 3 minutes.

PORK KAKUNI

I was hopping through Kugane's Rakuza District when some very angry kitchen workers grabbed me and dragged me into their establishment. They said I had eaten and fled without paying and had to work off my tab, but I told them I had never been there before! And they called me Gyodo although that is definitely not my name, no, no. But I ended up learning how to make a good pork kakuni so it worked out very nicely.

Difficulty: Easy · **Prep Time:** 1 hour · **Cook Time:** 4 hours
Yield: 4 servings · **Dietary Notes:** Dairy-free

Equipment: Medium pan, plate, medium pot, whisk, medium saucepan

Olive oil

2 pounds (1 kg) pork belly, cut into large cubes

3-inch (7.5-cm) piece of ginger, peeled and cut in half

3 scallions, cut in half

1 fennel bulb, quartered

Braising Sauce

2 cups (500 ml) dashi

¼ cup (60 ml) sake

¼ cup (60 ml) mirin

⅓ cup (80 ml) soy sauce

¼ cup (60 g) granulated sugar

3 tablespoons (40 g) firmly packed brown sugar

1. Line a plate with two layers of paper towels. In a pan over medium-high heat, warm 1 teaspoon of oil. Add the pork belly and cook until all sides have browned, about 10 minutes. Transfer the pork belly to the paper towel–lined plate and pat dry to remove any excess oil.

2. Transfer the pork belly to a pot. Add the ginger, scallions, and fennel quarters the pot. Fill with enough water to just cover all the ingredients. Set the pot over medium-high heat and bring to a boil. Reduce the heat and simmer until the pork has softened, 2 to 3 hours.

3. Strain the pork and pat dry. In a medium saucepan over medium-high, whisk together the dashi, sake, mirin, soy sauce, granulated sugar, and brown sugar. Add the pork belly. Bring to a boil, then reduce to a simmer and simmer for 1 hour, occasionally turning the pork belly to cover all sides in the sauce.

RARE ROAST BEEF

There are many dzo in the Azim Steppe, but I never had a reason to cook with dzo meat until now. Unfortunately, I am not much of a hunter, so I had to trade with an Auri hunter to get the ingredients for this recipe. The Au Ra are just as good at bargaining as we Namazu, regrettably, and I had to do a fair bit of fishing to make up the cost. But this roast beef recipe is worth the trouble!

Difficulty: Medium · **Prep Time:** 2 hour · **Rest Time:** 48 hours · **Cook Time:** 3½ hours
Yield: 4 servings · **Dietary Notes:** N/A

Equipment: Wire rack, 9-by-13-inch (23-by-33-cm) deep baking dish, small bowl, whisk, aluminum foil, small pot, meat thermometer

3 pounds (1.5 kg) bottom round roast
3 tablespoons (50 g) salt
2 teaspoons pepper
1 tablespoon dried rosemary
2 teaspoons dried thyme
5 garlic cloves, finely minced
5 mint leaves, finely chopped
1 teaspoon ground fennel
2 tablespoons whole-grain mustard
2 tablespoons olive oil
3 celery stalks (110 g), cut into large chunks
1 fennel bulb, cut into large chunks
3 shallots, cut into large chunks
3 carrots, cut into large chunks
2 rosemary sprigs
2 thyme sprigs

Gravy
Drippings from pan
4 tablespoons (60 g) butter
¼ cup (45 g) flour
2½ cups (625 ml) beef broth
Salt
Pepper

1. Two days before you plan on roasting the beef, season the roast all over with salt, pepper, rosemary, and thyme, rubbing the seasonings in with your hands. Place the beef on a wire rack set on top of a baking sheet and refrigerate, uncovered for at least 48 hours.

2. Remove the roast from the refrigerator and let it come to room temperature for 1 hour. Place an oven rack in the lower third of the oven and preheat the oven to 225°F (110°C).

3. In a small bowl, combine the garlic, mint, ground fennel, mustard, and oil. Rub the roast all over with the mixture.

4. Place the celery, fennel, shallots, carrots, rosemary, and thyme in a deep baking dish. Place the roast directly on top of the vegetables, fat side up.

5. Roast until the meat registers 120°F (49°C) on a meat thermometer inserted into in the thickest area, about 3 hours. Remove from the oven, loosely cover with aluminum foil, and let rest for 30 minutes.

6. While the meat is resting, begin making the gravy. In a pot over medium-high heat, combine the drippings from the baking dish with the butter. Once the butter has melted, whisk in the flour. Slowly add the broth while whisking. It is very important that you add the broth slowly and whisk constantly. This will allow the gravy to become nice and thick. Bring to a boil, reduce the heat, and simmer until the gravy has thickened. Season with salt and pepper. Set aside and keep warm.

7. Raise the oven temperature to 500°F (260°C). Position an oven rack in the upper third of the oven. Remove the aluminum foil and place the meat in the oven. Cook until the fat begins to crisp up, 8 to 10 minutes.

8. Wrap the meat in aluminum foil again and let rest for 5 minutes, before slicing into ½-inch (12 mm) thick pieces. Serve with the gravy on the side.

STARLIGHT DODO

The Namazu festival is certainly my favorite festival of all, yes, yes, but if I were forced to choose another, it would definitely be the Starlight Celebration. I set up a stall in Gridania this past year hoping to see the Warrior of Light, but I was so busy preparing and serving this delicious Starlight dodo that I forgot! Mogria said she would help, but she ran off to play in the snow as soon as the festivities started.

Difficulty: Medium · **Prep Time:** 1 hour · **Rest Time:** 12 to 24 hours · **Cook Time:** 3 hours
Yield: 1 whole duck · **Dietary Notes:** Dairy-free

Equipment: Large pot, large mesh strainer, wire rack, 9-by-13-inch (23-by-33-cm) baking sheet, small bowl, whisk, basting/pastry brush, aluminum foil, butcher's twine

One 6-pound (3-kg) whole duck
Salt
Pepper
5 garlic cloves, crushed
1 shallot, halved
1 lemon, halved
1 small orange, halved
1 rosemary sprig

Glaze
½ cup (170 g) honey
1 tablespoon orange juice
1 tablespoon molasses

1. Remove the neck and trim the excess fat and skin from the duck. Place the duck, breast side up, in a mesh strainer set over a sink. In a large pot, bring about 6 cups (1.5 L) of water to a boil. Pour half of the water over the duck. Turn the duck over and pour the remaining water over it. This will tighten the skin.

2. Transfer the duck to a wire rack set on a baking sheet. Generously salt all parts of the duck. Tie the legs together with butcher's twine. Refrigerate the duck, uncovered, for 12 to 24 hours.

3. Preheat the oven to 350°F (180°C). Remove the duck from the refrigerator and pat dry. Season all parts of the duck with pepper. Stuff the duck cavity with garlic, shallot, lemon, orange, and rosemary. Place the duck, breast side up, back on the wire rack on the baking sheet. Bake in the oven for 1 hour. Turn the duck over and bake for another 25 minutes.

4. In a small bowl, combine the ingredients for the glaze. Remove the duck from the oven and brush the back with the glaze. Return to the oven and bake for another 25 minutes.

5. Remove the duck from the oven, turn it over, brush with the glaze, and return the duck to the oven. Bake for 20 minutes. Brush the duck once more with the glaze and bake until the duck registers 160°F (71°C) on a meat thermometer inserted into the breast. Remove the duck from the oven and wrap in aluminum foil. Let rest for 15 minutes before carving.

STUFFED CABBAGE ROLL

 When we were in Rhalgr's Reach, a Miqo'te named M'naago pulled me aside and asked if I had time to lend her a hand. She said that she had heard all Namazu are excellent craftsfish, but I informed her that my fins were made for cooking, yes, yes. She said it was perfect and handed me a request for some stuffed cabbage rolls. I had never made them before, but it seemed simple enough, so I made her a set and had some for myself too. She also handed me some weird yellow napkins, but they didn't do a good job cleaning my fins.

Difficulty: Easy · **Prep Time:** 45 minutes · **Cook Time:** 1½ hours
Yield: 10 rolls · **Dietary Notes:** Dairy-free

Equipment: Medium saucepan, large pot, 13-by-9-by-2-inch (33-by-23-by-5-cm) deep baking dish

Tomato Sauce
One 28-ounce (794-g) can crushed tomatoes
One 28-ounce (794-g) can tomato sauce
2 tablespoons sugar
1 tablespoon white vinegar
½ tablespoon salt
1 tablespoon basil
1 tablespoon oregano
1 tablespoon thyme
Pepper

1 head green cabbage
Olive oil
¾ onion, chopped
4 garlic cloves, minced
1 pound (500 g) ground lamb
1 cup (155 g) cooked rice
½ tablespoon salt
½ teaspoon pepper
1 tablespoon oregano
1 tablespoon basil

1. In a medium saucepan over medium-high heat, stir together the sauce ingredients and bring to a slight boil. Reduce the heat and simmer until the sauce thickens, about 20 minutes. Set aside.

2. Preheat the oven to 375°F (190°C). Bring a large pot of water to a boil. Remove any dark green leaves from the cabbage and cut about ½ inch (12 mm) off the bottom. Place the cabbage in the boiling water and boil until the cabbage softens, about 10 minutes. Carefully remove the cabbage from the water and run cold water over it. Remove 10 leaves from the cabbage and set aside. Chop the remaining cabbage and place in a deep baking dish.

3. In a small pan over medium-high heat, combine 1 teaspoon of oil and the onions. Cook until the onions have softened, about 5 minutes. Add the garlic and cook for another 2 minutes. Remove from the heat, transfer the mixture to a medium bowl, and let cool.

4. Add the lamb, rice, salt, pepper, oregano, and basil to the bowl with the onion and garlic and mix until just combined. Using your hands, divide the mixture into 10 equal portions.

5. To assemble the rolls, make a 1-inch (2.5-cm) cut into the stem of a cabbage leaf. Place one of the filling portions in the center of the leaf and shape it into a log. Roll the leaf up from the bottom, tucking the sides in, and wrap the leaf at the top. Place on top of the chopped cabbage in the baking pan, seam side down. Repeat with the remaining lamb portions and cabbage.

6. Cover the cabbage rolls with the tomato sauce. Bake until the filling is cooked, about 45 to 60 minutes.

TRAPPER'S QUICHE

I spoke with some hunters around Camp Dragonhead about where I could find an eft for a recipe I had in mind. They very kindly pointed me in the right direction. But the efts were much bigger than I expected! I thought they were going to be nice little lizards but neither Mogria nor I are fighters, no, no. I went back to town empty-handed, but the hunters told me of some vegetation nearby in an eft's diet that shares a similar taste, so I went with something far less perilous.

Difficulty: Medium · **Prep Time:** 15 minutes · **Cook Time:** 1½ hours
Yield: 6 servings · **Dietary Notes:** N/A

Equipment: Medium bowl, whisk, medium frying pan

3 eggs

¾ cup (180 ml) heavy cream

4 ounces (125 g) cream cheese, at room temperature

1 tablespoon fish sauce

¼ teaspoon nutmeg

1 tablespoon olive oil

1 king oyster mushroom, sliced

4 shiitake mushrooms, sliced

1 cluster of oyster mushrooms, sliced

1 shallot, sliced

3½ ounces (105 g) Gruyère cheese, grated

1 store-bought pie crust

6 Thai basil leaves

1. Preheat the oven to 350°F (180°C). In a bowl, whisk together the eggs, heavy cream, cream cheese, fish sauce, and nutmeg until well combined. In a medium pan over medium heat, add a tablespoon of oil and sauté the mushrooms and shallots. Cook until the mushrooms have softened and crisped slightly, about 10 minutes.

2. Scatter the Gruyère evenly around the bottom of the pie crust. Spread the mushrooms and Thai basil over the cheese. Carefully pour the egg mixture into the crust. Bake until set, 50 to 60 minutes. Transfer to a cooling rack and let cool for at least 10 minutes before cutting into wedges and serving.

SIDES

CHAWAN-MUSHI

A perky peddler in Rhalgr's Reach pulled us aside, excited to tell us all about the revitalized salt industry in Ala Mhigo. He was going on and on for so long that I honestly wasn't paying very much attention until he said it was thanks to the Warrior of Light that things were back to normal. Yes, yes, I said the Warrior of Light helped me get on the right track too, and he was happy to hear it. He told me all about some new dishes that made their way here from across the Ruby Sea because of the new salt trade routes and handed me something I had never had before, a savory pudding called chawan-mushi.

Difficulty: Hard · **Prep Time:** 15 minutes · **Cook Time:** 20 minutes
Yield: 4 servings · **Dietary Notes:** Dairy-free

Equipment: Fine-mesh strainer, small bowls, 4 chawan-mushi cups, pot with steamer basket and lid

1 chicken thigh, cut into bite-size pieces

2 tablespoons sake

2 teaspoons soy sauce

4 shrimp, shells removed, deveined, and cut in half

3 scallops, cut into four pieces each

2 shiitake mushrooms, sliced

Eight ⅛-inch (3-mm) pieces of kamaboko

4 tablespoons (60 g) ikura

4 mitsuba stalks

Custard

3 eggs

1¼ cups (310 ml) dashi stock

1 teaspoon sake

½ teaspoon salt

1 teaspoon soy sauce

1. Pour water into a pot to a depth of 2 inches (5 cm). Insert a steamer basket and set the pot over medium heat.

2. Place the chicken pieces, sake, and soy sauce in a small bowl. Let marinate for 10 minutes.

3. In a bowl, combine all the ingredients for the custard. Pass the mixture through a fine-mesh strainer several times to remove excess bubbles from the mixture.

> **Be sure not to over mix the ingredients. It will add too much air to the mixture, too many bubbles.**

4. Place a few pieces of chicken in each chawan-mushi cup. Top with the shrimp and scallops. Add the shiitake mushrooms and kamaboko.

5. Slowly pour the custard into each chawan-mushi cup until ¼ inch (6 mm) from the top. Pop any bubbles with a toothpick to keep the top smooth. Cover each of the cups.

6. Place each cup in the steamer basket and cover the pot with a lid. Reduce the heat to medium-low and steam until the custard is cooked through, about 20 minutes. The internal temperature of the custard should register 165°F (74°C) on a kitchen thermometer.

7. To serve, top each custard with a tablespoon of ikura and a mitsuba stalk.

CHEESE RISOTTO

There's a nice little tavern called the Coffer & Coffin out near Black Brush Station. It was full of mercenaries and miners on break, but everyone was pretty nice for never seeing a moogle and a Namazu traveling together before, kupo. Actually, based on the looks we got, I don't think they've ever seen a moogle or a Namazu ever. I was a bit hungry, and the owner whipped up a fantastic treat: a cheese risotto made with wine fresh from the tap. Even in the rougher parts of Hydaelyn, you never know when you'll find something delicious, kupo!

Difficulty: Medium · **Prep Time:** 15 minutes · **Cook Time:** 30 minutes
Yield: 6 servings · **Dietary Notes:** Vegetarian

Equipment: Medium saucepan, large frying pan, spatula

5 cups (1.25 L) chicken broth

1 rosemary sprig

1 bay leaf

3 tablespoons (45 g) butter

1 onion, diced

3 garlic cloves, minced

2 parsnips, peeled and minced

2 cups (425 g) arborio rice

½ cup (125 ml) white wine

¾ cup (200 g) cottage cheese

3-ounce (90-g) wedge Parmesan cheese, shredded

Salt

Pepper

Furikake

1. In a medium saucepan over medium-high heat, combine the chicken broth, rosemary, and bay leaf. Bring to a boil, then reduce the heat to low to keep the broth warm.

2. In a large pan over medium-high heat, melt the butter. Add the onion, garlic, and parsnips and cook, stirring occasionally, until softened, about 5 minutes. Add the arborio rice and stir to coat the rice with the butter. Sauté for 2 minutes, but do not let the rice brown.

3. Add the white wine and stir constantly until all of the liquid is absorbed. Slowly add the chicken broth in ½-cup (125-ml) increments. Stir until the broth is fully absorbed before adding more liquid. Repeat until all of the broth is stirred in.

4. Remove from the heat and stir in the cottage cheese and Parmesan. Season with salt and pepper.

5. Scoop generous portions into 6 bowls and top each with furikake.

The locals like to only use cottage cheese for their risotto, but I've found that the extra flavor from Parmesan cheese really elevates this dish.

IMAM BAYILDI

We met up with Lyse at Rhalgr's Reach. She was super busy with something that seemed urgent, so I just wanted to say hello, kupo, but she was really nice and made time for the two of us. I talked about why we were traveling, and she said she had just the thing to add to our book. She brought us to a food stall where they had Imam Bayildi, a tasty mix of veggies cooked in Doman eggplants. She said they reminded her of the alliances she's worked on forming and the dreams she had. It was a very nice meeting, kupo!

Difficulty: Medium · **Prep Time:** 30 minutes · **Cook Time:** 1½ hours
Yield: 6 servings · **Dietary Notes:** Vegan

Equipment: Baking sheet, 9-by-13-inch (23-by-33-cm) baking sheet, parchment paper, colander, 10-inch (25½-cm) pan

6 Italian eggplants
1 tablespoon salt
2 tablespoons olive oil
1 tablespoon dried thyme
½ teaspoon pepper

Filling

2 tablespoons olive oil
3 shallots, sliced
7 garlic cloves, chopped
2 carrots, peeled and chopped
1 large tomato, diced
1 tablespoon tomato paste
1 teaspoon sugar
½ teaspoon salt
1 teaspoon dried thyme
1 teaspoon ground pink peppercorns
¼ cup parsley, minced

1. Preheat the oven to 375°F (190°C). Slice each Italian eggplant almost in half, but without cutting all the way through. Carve out a bit of each half to create space for filling. Rub the eggplant with salt and let sit for 10 minutes.

2. Line a baking sheet with parchment paper. Wipe off the salt and dry off each of the eggplants. In a small bowl, combine the oil, thyme, and pepper. Using your hands, rub the eggplants all over with the oil mixture. Place on the prepared baking sheet. Bake until the eggplants begin to soften, about 30 minutes.

3. Transfer the eggplant to a colander, cut side down, and let drain for 15 minutes. Set the baking sheet aside until needed again.

4. In a pan over medium heat, warm the oil. Add the shallots and cook until softened, about 5 minutes. Add the garlic and carrots and cook for another 5 minutes. Add the remaining ingredients and stir together well. Reduce the heat and simmer for 15 minutes.

5. Reduce the oven temperature to 350°F (180°C). Transfer the drained eggplants back to the baking sheet. Fill each eggplant with the filling. Bake until the filling is slightly crisped, about 20 minutes.

MASHED POPOTOES

I had been cooped up in kitchens and taverns for too long, so I decided to get out to eastern Thanalan and put some of my gathering skills to use. I heard the region had lots of different kinds of popotoes and thought getting my fins dirty could give me some inspiration, yes, yes, but it was exhausting! By the time I got back, I didn't know what to do with all I gathered, so I just mashed them together and added some dairy to flavor it. Mogria said it tasted nice, so it'll have to do!

Difficulty: Easy · **Prep Time:** 15 minutes · **Cook Time:** 30 minutes
Yield: 3 servings · **Dietary Notes:** Dairy, Vegetarian

Equipment: Large pot, strainer, potato masher

1 pound (500 g) russet potatoes, peeled and chopped
8 garlic cloves
1 teaspoon salt
6 tablespoons (84 g) butter
½ cup (142 g) sour cream
5 ounces (142 g) cottage cheese
Salt
Pepper

1. In a large pot over high heat, combine the potatoes and garlic and add just enough water to cover the potatoes. Add the salt. Bring to a boil, then reduce the heat and simmer until the potatoes are tender, 15 to 20 minutes. Drain and set the potatoes aside.

2. Set the pot back on the stove over medium heat and add the butter, sour cream, and cottage cheese. Cook until the butter has fully melted. Add the potatoes and mash until smooth. Season with salt and pepper to taste.

MUSHROOM SAUTÉ

After I finished working at the Bismarck, it was suggested I stop by Rowena's café and ask a chef named Raulf if he had any ideas for my book. The Hyur with a bright pumpkin orange chef's outfit was happy to show me a few things around the kitchen, yes, yes, and after I brought up my plans for my cookbook, Raulf was shocked. He too had gotten help from the Warrior of Light and shared a mushroom sauté that the Warrior had brought him when he needed some assistance.

Difficulty: Easy · **Prep Time:** 15 minutes · **Cook Time:** 30 minutes
Yield: 6 servings · **Dietary Notes:** Vegetarian

Equipment: Medium frying pan, spatula

1 tablespoon olive oil

2 tablespoons butter

8 shiitake mushrooms, stems removed and sliced

6 baby portobello mushrooms, stems removed and sliced

1 cluster beech mushrooms, roughly chopped

1 king oyster mushroom, sliced

1 cluster of oyster mushrooms, roughly chopped

1 tablespoon rosemary, chopped

1 teaspoon salt

1. In a medium pan over medium-high heat, melt the butter with the oil. Add the mushrooms. Sauté until they have turned golden brown, about 10 to 15 minutes.

2. Remove from the heat and season with rosemary and salt.

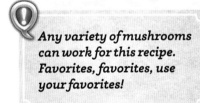

Any variety of mushrooms can work for this recipe. Favorites, favorites, use your favorites!

POPOTOES AU GRATIN

I do love swimming, yes, yes, but I've always been told to stay out of the Ruby Sea because of a legendary fish that eats Plainsfolk like they were popotoes. I had an idea that, if I were able to make a popoto dish tasty enough to satisfy the beast, maybe it would leave me alone and let me swim in the nice warm waters by Hells' Lid. But based on what I've heard, I'm going to need a lot more popotoes than what's in this dish.

Difficulty: Easy · **Prep Time:** 45 minutes · **Cook Time:** 1 hour
Yield: 6 to 8 servings · **Dietary Notes:** Vegetarian

Equipment: Medium saucepan, whisk, medium pan, spatula, 8-by-8-by-2-inch (21-by-21-by-5-cm) deep baking dish, aluminum foil, paper towel

Cream Filling
3 tablespoons (35 g) all-purpose flour
1 teaspoon dried oregano
½ teaspoon dried thyme
½ teaspoon ground mustard
½ teaspoon salt
1 teaspoon pepper
3 tablespoons (45 g) unsalted butter
6 garlic cloves, minced
2 ounces (60 g) cream cheese
1½ cups (375 ml) goat milk*

Caramelized Onions
1 tablespoon unsalted butter
1 tablespoon olive oil
1 onion, sliced
Salt

1¾ pounds (875 g) russet potatoes, peeled and sliced into ⅛-inch (3-mm) slices
Cream filling
Caramelized onions
Three ½-ounce (105-g) wedges Gruyère cheese, shredded
½-ounce (50-g) piece of cheddar cheese, shredded
1-ounce (30-g) wedge Parmesan cheese, shredded

*If you can't find goat's milk, any kind of dairy will work, yes, yes!

1. In a small bowl, combine the flour, oregano, thyme, ground mustard, salt, and pepper.

2. In a saucepan over medium-high heat, melt the butter. Add the garlic and cook until lightly golden brown, about 5 minutes.

3. Add the flour mixture to the pan and whisk together. Add the cream cheese and stir until well combined. After the butter, flour, and cream cheese have combined into a roux, slowly whisk in the goat milk until fully combined. Whisk continuously until the mixture thickens, then remove from the heat and set aside.

4. In a frying pan over medium heat, melt the butter with the oil. Add the onion and toss to coat with the oil. Cook the onions until they turn translucent, about 2 minutes.

5. Add the salt, stir, and reduce the heat to medium-low. Continue cooking, stirring occasionally, until the onions become golden and caramelized, 30 to 45 minutes. Remove from the heat and set aside.

6. Preheat the oven to 375°F (190°C). Spread one-third of the cream filling over the bottom of a baking dish. Top with a layer of potatoes, then spread the caramelized onions across the potatoes and then spread with another layer (but not all) of the cream filling. Top with more potatoes and the remaining cream. Cover the baking dish with aluminum foil and cook in the oven for 45 minutes.

7. Remove aluminum foil and top with the Gruyere, cheddar, and Parmesan. Place the dish back in the oven and cook for another 25 minutes.

The cheese can get greasy. To remove some of the grease, simply dab the top lightly with a paper towel.

8. Turn on the broiler and broil until the cheese lightly browns.

RATATOUILLE

On my way to Gridania, some nice people on the airship asked why we were traveling and suggested we visit the Botanists' Guild. Very correct, very helpful! The giant pumpkins, fields of fresh veggies—everything was better than I expected. I was so impressed by all the produce that I asked if they knew of any meals that highlighted all the great veggies, and the guild leader, a Lalafell named Fufucha, suggested a fresh ratatouille. There's no way I'm fitting those pumpkins in this dish, though, so I had to use smaller vegetables, yes, yes!

Difficulty: Easy · **Prep Time:** 45 minutes · **Cook Time:** 1 hour
Yield: 4 servings · **Dietary Notes:** Vegan

Equipment: 9-by-13-inch (23-by-33-cm) baking sheet, aluminum foil, large bowl, small bowl

Nonstick cooking spray

1 eggplant, cubed

2 zucchini, cubed

2 squash, cubed

2 bell peppers, seeded and cut into chunks

1 onion, cut into chunks

1 cup (150 g) cherry tomatoes

½ cup (125 ml) plus 2 tablespoons olive oil

1 teaspoon dried thyme

2 teaspoons lavender

5 garlic cloves, minced

1 teaspoon salt

½ teaspoon pepper

1. Preheat the oven to 400°F (200°C). Line a large baking sheet with aluminum foil. Spray the foil with nonstick cooking spray and set aside.

2. Place all the vegetables in a large bowl and toss until mixed together. In a small bowl, combine ½ cup (65 g) oil, thyme, lavender, garlic, salt, and pepper. Pour the oil mixture over the vegetables and toss until well coated.

3. Transfer the vegetables to the prepared baking sheet and spread into an even layer. Roast for 20 minutes, then stir the vegetables on the baking sheet and roast for another 20 minutes. Stir the vegetables once more, reduce the heat to 350°F (180°C), and roast for another 20 minutes.

4. Transfer the roasted vegetables to a large bowl and toss in the remaining 2 tablespoons oil.

 SPINACH SAUTÉ

After all the different proteins I learned to work with in La Noscea and Thanalan, I appreciate the lighter recipes that the Black Shroud's cuisine has to offer. I may be a Namazu, yes, yes, but my palette is refined and I appreciate all sorts of vegetables with my meal. I was a little confused walking through Gridania when I overheard someone mention something about leaf meats? Maybe I misheard them. Surely, surely, meat doesn't grow on trees here.

Difficulty: Easy · **Prep Time:** 15 minutes · **Cook Time:** 30 minutes
Yield: 6 servings · **Dietary Notes:** Vegetarian

Equipment: Medium pot, small frying pan, whisk

1 pound (500 g) gai lan, stem and
  leaves split
1 teaspoon sesame oil
2 teaspoon peanut oil
6 garlic cloves, sliced
1 tablespoon fresh ginger, minced
2 tablespoons black vinegar
1 teaspoon soy sauce
1 tablespoon honey

1. Bring a pot of water to a boil. Place the gai lan stems in the pot and simmer for 2 minutes. Transfer the gai lan stems to a plate. Place the gai lan leaves in the water and cook for 1 minute. Transfer the leaves to the same plate as the stems.

2. In a small pan over medium-high heat, combine the sesame oil and peanut oil and let heat up for about 1 minute. Add the garlic and ginger and cook until fragrant, about 2 minutes. Transfer to a bowl. Add the black vinegar, soy sauce, and honey to the bowl and whisk together. Pour over the gai lan and serve.

DESSERTS

APPLE STRUDEL

We found a large tavern in the middle of the South Shroud called Buscarron's Druthers that had all sorts of food and drink from the area. But we had been walking all day and I kept seeing apple trees everywhere I went, so I asked if they had something with apples in it. Sitting outside in the shade, enjoying the sounds of birds, and a fresh apple strudel delivered to the table? No better way to enjoy an afternoon, kupo!

If Golden Apples are unavailable, use any harder apple variety you've harvested. Make sure to use three of them!

Difficulty: Easy · **Prep Time:** 45 minutes · **Cook Time:** 45 minutes
Yield: 2 strudels (8 servings) · **Dietary Notes:** Dairy, Vegetarian

Equipment: Large bowl, large frying pan, large fine-mesh strainer, parchment paper, knife, 9-by-13-inch (23-by-33-cm) baking sheet

2 Granny Smith apples, peeled, cored, and diced

1 Honey Crisp apple, peeled, cored, and diced

1 tablespoon lemon juice

2 tablespoons birch syrup

2 tablespoons granulated sugar

¼ cup (60 g) firmly packed light brown sugar

1 vanilla bean, seeds scraped

½ teaspoon ground cardamom

1 teaspoon ground cinnamon

2 tablespoons cornstarch

2 tablespoons unsalted butter

2 sheets of puff pastry, thawed

1 egg

1 tablespoon water

1. Preheat the oven to 400°F (200°C). In a large bowl, combine the apples, lemon juice, birch syrup, granulated sugar, brown sugar, vanilla seeds, cardamom, cinnamon, and cornstarch. In a large pan over medium-high heat, melt the butter. Add the apple mixture and cook until the apples become tender and the liquid has thickened, 10 to 15 minutes.

2. Transfer the cooked apples into a large fine-mesh strainer and drain the liquid. Transfer the apples to a bowl and let cool completely.

3. Unfold a sheet of puff pastry on a piece of parchment paper. Place half of the filling in the center third of the puff pastry. Using a sharp knife, cut 8 horizontal strips on the edges of the outer thirds of the puff pastry. Cross the strips over the filling by alternating from the left and right side. Repeat until all the strips are crossed and the filling is sealed. Trim off any excess dough. Repeat this step with the other puff pastry and remaining filling.

4. In a small bowl, whisk together the egg and water. Brush each of the braided puff pastries with the egg wash. Bake until golden brown, 25 to 30 minutes. Transfer to a wire rack and let cool completely before cutting.

CHEESE SOUFFLÉ

Head chef Doesfalksyn pulled me into the kitchen and told me to whip up his famous cheese soufflé. I hadn't yet made something so challenging, but I was really proud of how well it turned out, yes, yes. I asked the head chef where the order was going and he said "Ah, ye' can leave it right here. This dish always gets me head on straight." He then offered me a piece. Wow, wow, the delicate sponginess paired with the booming flavor definitely helped me stay focused for the rest of my shift.

Difficulty: Hard · **Prep Time:** 45 minutes · **Cook Time:** 1½ hour
Yield: 1 Cake (8 servings) · **Dietary Notes:** Dairy, Vegetarian

Equipment: 9-inch (23-cm) springform pan, parchment paper, aluminum foil, double-boiler, 13-by-9-by-2-inch (33-by-23-by-5-cm) deep baking dish, medium saucepan, small bowl, stand mixer, spatula, basting/pastry brush

2 tablespoons butter, at room temperature, plus butter for greasing

12 ounces (342 g) cream cheese, at room temperature

½ cup (125 ml) milk

¼ cup (60 ml) heavy cream

¼ cup (60 ml) maple syrup

6 eggs, separated

1½ tablespoons cornstarch

Pinch of salt

1 teaspoon lemon juice

⅔ cup (90 g) cake flour

¼ teaspoon cream of tartar

½ cup (100 g) sugar

Hot water

Honey

1. Lightly grease a springform pan with butter. Cut out a round piece of parchment paper to line the bottom of the pan with. Cut out another piece of parchment paper to line the inside edge of the pan. Wrap the outside of the springform pan in aluminum foil. This prevents water from seeping into the pan while the soufflé is cooking.

2. Place a rack in the lower third of the oven and preheat the oven to 325°F (165°C). Fill the bottom pot of a double-boiler with water and bring to a simmer over medium-high heat. Place the cream cheese, butter, milk, and heavy cream in the top pot and set it over the simmering water. Warm the cream cheese mixture, stirring gently, until the mixture is completely smooth.

3. Remove the double-boiler from the heat and add the maple syrup. Stir well. Set aside and let cool completely.

4. In a small bowl, stir together the egg yolks, cornstarch, salt, and lemon juice.

5. Add the egg yolk mixture to the cooled cream cheese mixture. Stir until completely combined. Whisk in the cake flour until combined.

6. Place the egg whites in the bowl of a stand mixer fitted with the whisk attachment. Whisk on high speed until the egg whites begin to foam. Add the cream of tartar and sugar and whisk until the egg whites reach stiff peaks.

7. Transfer a third of the egg white mixture to the bowl with the cream cheese mixture. Whisk until well incorporated. Add another third of the egg white mixture and carefully fold in until well combined. Gently fold in the remaining third of the egg white mixture until there are no streaks and everything is mixed well.

Continued on next page

8. Carefully pour the batter into the prepared springform pan. Lift the pan and bang it lightly on the countertop several times to remove any excess air bubbles from the batter.

9. Place the springform pan in a large, deep baking dish. Pour hot water into the baking dish until it reaches about halfway up the sides of the pan. Make sure no water is seeping into the pan.

10. Place the baking dish on the rack in the lower third of the oven and bake for 45 minutes. Reduce the heat to 275°F (135°C) and bake until the soufflé top is browned, another 35 to 40 minutes. If the top of the cake has not browned, raise the heat to 325°F (165°C) and cook for another 2 to 3 minutes.

11. Let the soufflé cool, then remove the springform pan. Carefully brush the top with honey. This soufflé can be enjoyed at room temperature or chilled.

CHOCOBO CAKE*

Did you know that there is chocobo racing at the Manderville Gold Saucer? We went to see the races and I couldn't believe how fast some of those chocobos can go! Apparently, some of the riders train their chocobo by dangling decadent pieces of cake in front of them, but that just seems cruel. If I were training a chocobo, I'd just feed it cake every day. Gyohan said my idea was silly and it would just make the chocobo fat, but I might try it and see what happens anyway, kupo.

Difficulty: Hard · **Prep Time:** 2 hours · **Cook Time:** 45 minutes
Yield: 1 Cake (8 servings) · **Dietary Notes:** Vegetarian

Equipment: Two 8-inch (20-cm) cake pans, parchment paper, small bowls, stand mixer, offset or icing spatula, piping bag, drop flower decorating tip

Cake
Nonstick cooking spray
3 cups (375 g) cake flour
½ teaspoon ground cardamom
1 tablespoon baking powder
1 teaspoon salt
1 cup (250 g) unsalted butter, room temperature
1½ cups (335 g) beet sugar
2 whole eggs
2 egg whites
1 tablespoon vanilla extract
1 vanilla bean, seeds scraped
1¼ cups (310 g) oat milk

Syrup
3 tablespoons (45 g) granulated sugar
2 tablespoons (28 g) water
2 tablespoons (28 g) raspberry liqueur

Whipped Cream Frosting
4 cups (840 g) heavy cream
2 teaspoons vanilla extract
6 tablespoons (54 g) powdered sugar

To assemble the cake
2 cake layers
Whipped cream frosting
10 to 14 strawberries, top removed and cut in half
8 to 10 strawberries, top removed

1. Preheat the oven to 350°F (180°C). Spray the cake pans with nonstick cooking spray, then line each pan with parchment paper.

2. In a bowl, stir together the flour, cardamom, baking powder, and salt and set aside. In a large bowl, combine the butter and sugar and mix until smooth. Add the eggs, egg whites, vanilla extract, and vanilla bean seeds.

3. Add half of the flour mixture to the butter and sugar mixture and mix well. Add the oat milk and mix until smooth. Add the remaining flour mixture and mix until just combined.

4. Divide the batter equally between the 2 prepared cake pans. Lift each of the pans and bang them lightly on the countertop several times to remove any large air bubbles from the batter. Bake the cakes until a toothpick inserted into the center of the cakes comes out clean, 40 to 45 minutes.

5. Let the cakes cool in the pans for 5 minutes, then remove the cakes from the pans and transfer them to a wire rack. Be sure to remove the parchment paper from the cakes and let them cool completely, at least 1 hour.

6. In a microwave-safe bowl, combine all the syrup ingredients. Microwave for 15 seconds at a time, whisking between each interval, until the sugar has dissolved. Set aside until you are ready to assemble the cake.

7. In the bowl of a stand mixer fitted with the whisk attachment, combine all the whipped cream frosting ingredients and whisk on high speed until the frosting reaches a state between soft and stiff peaks. Getting the frosting a little past soft peaks makes it a bit sturdier on the cake. If you aren't ready to assemble the cake, cover the frosting bowl with plastic wrap and place in the refrigerator.

Continued on next page

8. Level the cake layers by slicing the top bump off with a serrated knife. Place one of the layers on a serving plate.

9. Brush the top of the layer with the syrup. Spread a layer of frosting about ¼ inch (6 mm) thick evenly over the syrup. Distribute the halved strawberries evenly over the frosting, then top with more frosting, just enough to cover the strawberries.

10. Brush syrup over the cut side of the other cake layer. Place the layer, cut side down, on top of the frosting. If you still have syrup left, brush the top side with it.

11. Prepare a piping bag with a drop flower tip. Transfer one-fourth of the frosting into the piping bag and set aside. Using an offset spatula or an icing spatula, spread the remaining frosting evenly all over the cake. To smooth the sides, run an offset spatula edge against the side as you rotate the cake.

12. Use the frosting in the piping bag to make little whipped-cream peaks around the edge of the cake. Place the whole strawberries in a circle around the center of the top of the cake.

*This recipe does not have an equivalent in-game item.

I recommend letting this cake sit covered in the refrigerator for at least 1 hour before cutting into it! It can be stored in the refrigerator for up to three days.

COFFEE BISCUIT

I overheard the Scions talking about someone's love of coffee biscuits and I thought I also should have some. I asked Gyohan to learn how to make them so we could also love coffee biscuits. They were so tasty that we both ate too many and I could barely fly, kupo! Next time, we should split one instead.

Difficulty: Easy · **Prep Time:** 45 minutes · **Rest Time:** 1 hour · **Cook Time:** 15 minutes
Yield: 24 cookies · **Dietary Notes:** Vegetarian

Equipment: Small bowl, medium bowl, large bowl, three 9-by-13-inch (23-cm-by-33-cm) baking sheets, parchment paper

1 tablespoon espresso powder

1 tablespoon hot water

2½ cups (390 g) all-purpose flour

¼ cup (45 g) whole-wheat flour

¼ teaspoon salt

1 teaspoon baking powder

1 cup (250 g) unsalted butter, room temperature

½ cup (130 g) beet sugar

½ cup (105 g) firmly packed brown sugar

2 eggs

1 teaspoon vanilla extract

8 ounces (250 g) dark chocolate chips

1. In a small bowl, whisk together the espresso powder and hot water. In a medium bowl, combine the all-purpose flour, whole-wheat flour, salt, and baking powder.

2. In a large bowl, combine the butter, beet sugar, and brown sugar and mix until smooth. Add the eggs, vanilla, and espresso powder mixture. Slowly mix in the flour mixture until the dough just comes together. Fold in the chocolate chips.

3. Line two baking sheets with parchment paper. Divide the dough into balls of approximately 2½ tablespoons (50 grams) and place on a prepared baking sheet. Using the palm of your hand, gently press each ball down on the parchment paper to make a thick disk. Place the baking sheets in the refrigerator for 1 hour.

4. Preheat the oven to 350°F (180°C). Line a baking sheet with parchment paper. Place the cookies on the baking sheet with 2 inches (5 cm) of space between each. Bake the cookies until they have slightly spread and the edges are golden, 15 to 20 minutes. Let the cookies completely cool.

DANGO

There are all sorts of interesting people you can meet while traveling, yes, yes! We were passing through Isari along the Ruby Sea when I came across a mountain of a monk enjoying what he called dango. He was much fun to talk to, yes, yes, and said the dango reminded him of a friend he once had. I asked if I could try some, but he handed me a stick without a green dango because he knew of the Namazu's weakness to tea. Well, now I need to get back to the kitchen and make some for myself! With extra green tea!

Difficulty: Easy · **Prep Time:** 45 minutes · **Cook Time:** 30 minutes

Yield: 4 servings · **Dietary Notes:** Vegan

Equipment: Medium pot, medium bowl, 9-by-13-inch (23-by-33-cm) baking sheet, bamboo skewers

¾ cups (120 g) joshinko rice flour

⅓ cup (100 g) plus 1 tablespoon shiratamako rice flour

½ tablespoon sugar

½ cup (125 ml) hot water

1 teaspoon matcha

2 tablespoons (4 g) freeze-dried strawberries, finely ground

1 drop pink food dye (optional)

1. In a bowl, combine the joshinko, shiratamako, and sugar. Slowly pour in half the hot water and stir. Add more water as needed. The consistency of the dough should feel like an earlobe. Lightly knead the dough until completely smooth.

   It is very important to keep the dough from drying out! Keep your fins and hands lightly wet during the whole process.

2. Divide the dough into three equal portions. Cover two of the portions with a damp kitchen towel. Knead the matcha into the third portion until combined. Then, place it under the damp kitchen towel. Knead in the ground strawberries and food dye into the second portion until combined. Place under the damp kitchen towel.

3. Divide each portion into four (about 20 to 25 grams each) pieces. With your hands, lightly moisten and shape the dough into smooth balls. Transfer to a plate and cover with a damp towel to keep the dough from drying out.

4. Bring a pot with water to a boil. Fill a bowl with ice and water. Add the dango to the pot. Stir the dango so they don't stick to the bottom. Once the dango start to float, after 3 or 4 minutes, they are done. Transfer to the ice water bath. Let cool for about 2 minutes.

5. Lightly moisten a baking sheet with water. Drain the dango and transfer to the prepared baking sheet. Thread a matcha dango onto a bamboo skewer, followed by a white dango, and top with a strawberry dango. Repeat with the remaining dango. Serve immediately.

KUPO NUTS*

Mogria and I have had quite the culinary cruise around Hydaelyn, but she never stops talking about kupo nuts, yes, yes. Any time we find any, she eats them before I get to try them, so I decided to make my own kupo nut recipe instead. I based all of the flavors and textures on the way Mogria talks about kupo nuts, so I am most certain, most positive, that these taste just like the real thing.

Difficulty: Easy · **Prep Time:** 1 hour · **Rest Time:** 1 hour
Yield: 18 to 20 balls · **Dietary Notes:** Vegetarian

Equipment: Food processor, medium bowl, 9-by-13-inch (23-by-33-cm) baking sheet, parchment paper

⅔ cup (85 g) walnuts
½ cup (75 g) cashews
¼ cup (40 g) pistachios
¾ cup (185 g) almond butter
1 tablespoon honey
1 tablespoon maple syrup
½ cup (62 g) ground flaxseed
1 tablespoon chia seeds
2 teaspoons flaky salt
½ cup (90 g) dried cherries
4½ ounces (140 g) dark chocolate chips
3 tablespoons (30 g) white sesame seeds
3 tablespoons (30 g) black sesame seeds

1. Place the walnuts, cashews, and pistachios in a food processor. Pulse until the nuts are crumbled. Add the almond butter, honey, maple syrup, ground flax seed, chia seeds, flaky salt, dried cherries, and chocolate chips and blend until completely combined.

2. Line a baking sheet with parchment paper. Transfer the mixture into a bowl. Form 1 tablespoon (35 grams) of the mixture into a ball. Place the ball on the prepared baking sheet. Repeat with the rest of the mixture.

3. Fill a resealable bag with the white and black sesame seeds. Working with one ball at a time, put the ball in the bag and toss it until it is coated with sesame seeds. Place each ball back on the prepared baking sheet, spaced about ¼ inch (.6 cm) apart. Chill in the refrigerator for 1 hour.

4. Transfer the balls to an airtight container. The kupo nuts can be stored in the refrigerator for up to 2 weeks.

*This recipe does not have an equivalent in-game item.

Gyohan, what are all these ingredients, kupo? **Kupo nuts are just KUPO NUTS!**

PAPANASI

This is a recipe I learned before setting off on my journey with Mogria. The Xaela were fighting on the Azim Steppe as usual recently, but this time they all seemed to be friends afterwards. I never thought I'd see the day where the tribes were working together, and it made me wonder if I could make a dessert with different layers that work the same way. At least, I think that's where the idea came from? Or perhaps I just got hungry and threw random things together. Yes, yes, Namazu inspiration can come from anywhere.

Difficulty: Medium · **Prep Time:** 1 hour · **Rest Time:** 45 minutes
Yield: 6 to 8 papanasi · **Dietary Notes:** Dairy, Vegetarian

Equipment: Small airtight containers, medium saucepan, medium bowl, large bowl, medium deep pot, deep-fry thermometer, fine-mesh spoon

Sour Cream Sauce

1 cup (227 g) sour cream

2 teaspoons vanilla extract

1 tablespoon lemon juice

2 tablespoons powdered sugar

Rolanberry Jam

¾ cup (170 g) strawberries, hulled and chopped

¾ cup (170 g) frozen cherries

½ cup (86 g) raspberries, chopped

½ cup (100 g) sugar

2 tablespoons lemon juice

Doughnuts

2¼ cups (310 g) all-purpose flour, plus more as needed, plus flour for dusting

½ cup (118 g) sugar

1 teaspoon salt

1½ teaspoons baking powder

2 cups (500 g) ricotta cheese

2 eggs

1 tablespoon vanilla extract

1 tablespoon rum (optional)

Peanut oil

1. In a bowl, mix all the ingredients for the sour cream sauce until smooth. The sauce can be stored in an airtight container in the refrigerator for up to 1 week.

2. In a saucepan over medium-high heat, combine all the ingredients for the jam and bring to a boil. Once the sugar has dissolved, smash the fruit. Reduce the heat and simmer until the mixture reduces and thickens, 20 to 25 minutes.

3. Remove from the heat and transfer to an airtight container to cool. Once cooled, chill in the refrigerator for at least 3 hours before serving. The jam can be stored in an airtight container in the refrigerator for up to 1 week.

4. In a medium bowl, combine the flour, sugar, salt, and baking powder. In a large bowl, combine the ricotta cheese, eggs, vanilla, and rum, if using. Add the flour mixture to the ricotta cheese mixture and mix together. The end result will be sticky but workable in your hands. If it is too sticky, add more flour, a little at a time, until the desired texture is reached.

5. Generously flour a work surface and your hands. Divide the dough into 8 portions and place on the floured surface.

6. Using your hands, shape 1 portion into a ball. Pinch the center of the ball to create a hole, giving the ball a doughnut shape. Set the doughnut aside on the floured surface. Repeat with the remaining portions.

7. Line a plate with two layers of paper towels and set it by the stovetop. Pour the peanut oil into a deep pot to a depth of 2 inches (5 cm). Set the pot over medium heat and heat the oil until it registers 350°F (180°C) on a deep-fry thermometer. Place the doughnuts in the oil, making sure not to overcrowd the pot, and cook for 4 minutes. Turn the doughnuts over and cook for 2 to 3 minutes longer. Remove the doughnuts from the oil and place them on the paper towel-lined plate. Repeat with the remaining doughnuts. The oil temperature might drop between each fry, so be sure to bring the oil temperature back up to 350°F (180°C) before frying the next batch of doughnuts.

8. To serve, place a doughnut on a plate and generously top with the sour cream sauce and rolanberry jam.

PRINCESS PUDDING

I had to learn this dessert while working at the Bismarck in preparation for the Starlight Celebration, but I didn't understand why the design was so particular. Another chef said it was supposed to resemble something called Princess Pudding, but I never knew dessert could be royalty, no, no. And a dessert walking around? I sure hope I never run into a noble sweet like that—it sounds terrible.

Difficulty: Hard · **Prep Time:** 45 minutes · **Cook Time:** 30 minutes
Yield: 4 cakes · **Dietary Notes:** Dairy, Vegetarian

Equipment: Medium saucepan, whisk, bowl, parchment paper, plastic wrap, small bowl, medium bowl, four 6-ounce (180 ml) ramekins

Ganache Filling

2½ ounces (75 g) dark chocolate

2 tablespoons heavy cream

2 teaspoons butter

Pinch of salt

Cake

5 ounces (155 g) dark chocolate

⅓ cup (90 g) unsalted butter, plus butter for the ramekins

2 eggs

2 egg yolks

2 tablespoons granulated sugar

2 tablespoons firmly packed brown sugar

2 teaspoons amaretto

¼ cup (45 g) all-purpose flour

¼ teaspoon salt

Whipped cream

Berries or other fresh fruit

1. In a medium saucepan over medium-low heat, combine the ingredients for the filling and cook until the chocolate has melted and is smooth. Transfer to an airtight container to cool. Refrigerate the filling for at least 1 hour, or until cool enough the handle with your hands.

2. Place a piece of parchment paper on a plate. Divide the ganache into 4 equal portions. Using your hands, shape each portion into a ball. Place the balls on the prepared plate and cover with plastic wrap. Freeze the balls for 15 to 20 minutes.

3. In a medium saucepan over medium-low heat, combine the chocolate and butter. Cook, stirring occasionally, until the chocolate is melted. Remove from the heat and let cool completely.

4. Preheat the oven to 375°F (190°C). Prepare four 6-ounce (180-ml) ramekins by generously greasing the insides with butter.

5. In a large bowl, whisk the eggs, egg yolks, granulated sugar, and brown sugar until pale and thickened. Whisk in the cooled chocolate and amaretto. Fold in the flour and salt until just combined.

6. Fill each of the ramekins just under halfway with the batter. Place one ball of ganache in the center of the batter in each of the ramekins. Cover with the remaining batter.

 Be sure to not overfill these! Fill them up to about ¼ inch from the top!

7. Transfer the ramekins to a baking sheet. Bake until the cakes are cooked through, about 15 minutes. Let cool for 2 minutes. Run a knife around the inside edge of the ramekin, then invert the ramekin on a plate to remove the cake. Serve with a dollop of whipped cream and fresh fruit.

ROLANBERRY CHEESECAKE

This cheesecake is one of the desserts I learned to make while training at the Bismarck. When the recipe said to swirl the purée with the filling, I spent a lot of time drawing a very good looking Namazu face. I showed the head chef my results, proud as I could be, but he considered his words carefully. "I like yer passion, I do" he told me, "but drawin' a goobbue on top will just startle the patrons." I was trying to make a Namazu! No, no, I must work on my artistic abilities after this book is done. For now, a swirl will have to do.

Difficulty: Hard · **Prep Time:** 45 minutes · **Cook Time:** 1 hour
Yield: 1 cheesecake · **Dietary Notes:** Vegetarian

Equipment: Blender, mesh strainer, medium saucepan, food processor, 9-inch (23-cm) springform pan, aluminum foil, 13-by-9-by-2-inch (33-by-23-by-5-cm) deep baking dish, small bowl, mixer (hand or stand), kitchen thermometer

Rolanberry Sauce

¾ cup (170 g) strawberries, hulled and chopped

¾ cup (170 g) frozen cherries

½ cup (86 g) raspberries, chopped

½ cup (100 g) sugar

2 tablespoons lemon juice

Crust

1¾ cups (175 g) graham crackers

3 tablespoons (45 g) sugar

6 tablespoons (90 g) butter, melted

Filling

24 ounces (750 g) cream cheese, at room temperature

1¼ cups (250 g) sugar

1 teaspoon salt

1 teaspoon vanilla extract

1 vanilla bean, seeds scraped

1 cup (220 g) sour cream

¼ cup (65 g) heavy cream

3 eggs

1. Combine all the ingredients for the sauce in a blender and blend until smooth. Pour the mixture through a mesh strainer into a saucepan. Set the saucepan over medium-high heat and bring to a simmer for 5 minutes. Transfer to an airtight container, let cool, then refrigerate until needed.

> *There will be a lot of extra sauce, yes, yes! You only need a small amount for the cheesecake, but I suggest chilling the extra to add when serving!*

2. Preheat the oven to 350°F (180°C). Place the graham crackers in a food processor and pulse until smooth. Add the sugar and melted butter and mix until well combined.

3. Wrap the outside of a springform pan with a double layer of aluminum foil. Scrape the graham cracker crumb mixture into the prepared pan. Press the crust down until it is flat and even. Bake the crust for 10 minutes. Remove from the oven and set aside. Reduce the heat to 325°F (165°C).

4. In a large bowl, stir the cream cheese until smooth and fluffy. Stir in the sugar, salt, vanilla extract, and vanilla bean seeds. Add the sour cream and heavy cream and whisk until well combined. Add the eggs to the mixture, one at a time, stirring after each addition. Mix until everything is well combined. Pour the filling into the springform pan.

5. Place drops of the rolanberry sauce on the filling. Dip a toothpick into each drop and swirl the sauce with the filling. Place the pan in a deep baking dish. Pour hot water into the baking dish until it reaches about halfway up the side of the springform pan. Make sure water isn't seeping into the springform pan. Bake the cheesecake until the top has set, and the cheesecake registers 150°F (66°C) on a kitchen thermometer, 60 to 75 minutes.

6. Turn off heat and let the cheesecake sit in the oven for 30 minutes. Transfer the cheesecake to a wire rack and cool completely. Refrigerate the cheesecake overnight and serve the next day. When removing the cheesecake from the springform pan, run a knife along the inside edge before undoing the pan. Serve with additional rolanberry sauce.

SESAME COOKIES

I asked Gyohan if we could go out of our way to see something in the Dravanian hinterlands. I heard the Warrior of Light had fought a primal larger than life and wanted to see it for myself, so he made some cookies for the trip. Gyohan was so shocked by how large the mechanical fortress was that he put one foot forward too far and almost fell off a cliff, but I pulled him back. He was so thankful that I suggested he could forward his gratitude with more cookies when we got back.

Difficulty: Medium · **Prep Time:** 30 minutes · **Rest Time:** 1 hour · **Cook Time:** 15 to 20 minutes
Yield: 24 cookies · **Dietary Notes:** Dairy, Vegetarian

Equipment: Food processor (or mortar and pestle), small bowl, large bowl, two 9-by-13-inch (23-by-33-cm) baking sheets, parchment paper

⅓ cup (43 g) plus 1 tablespoon black sesame seeds
1½ cups (235 g) all-purpose flour
½ cup (68 g) almond flour
1 teaspoon salt
1 cup (250 g) unsalted butter
1 cup (125 g) powdered sugar
2 tablespoons honey

1. Preheat the oven to 325°F (165°C). In a food processor (or using a mortar and pestle), grind the ⅓ cup black sesame seeds until about half of the seeds are ground.

2. In a small bowl, combine the all-purpose flour, almond flour, the 1 tablespoon black sesame seeds, and the salt. In a large bowl, combine the butter and powdered sugar. Add the honey and mix until well combined. Add the flour mixture and mix well.

3. Line two baking sheets with parchment paper, then dust the parchment paper with flour. (Do not use nonstick cooking spray as it will cause the cookies to spread too much.) Scoop up a tablespoon of the dough and use your hands to roll it into a ball. Place the ball on one of the prepared baking sheets, then gently press down on the ball to make a disk about 2½ inches (6 cm) wide. Repeat with the remaining dough. Place the baking sheet in the refrigerator for 1 hour.

4. Bake until the cookies have slightly spread and the edges are golden, 15 to 20 minutes. Let the cookies completely cool.

DRINKS

CRIMSON CIDER

I learned of a drink with the same name in both the Ala Mhigan Resistance and the Doman Liberation Front, but different places gave me different recipes! Very strange, very strange. Perhaps the two groups have different preferences in spirits? I made both recipes in order to decide which I found to have the better flavor, but I drank too much and don't remember, so you can decide for yourself, yes, yes!

Difficulty: Easy · **Prep Time:** 15 minutes · **Cook Time:** 40 minutes
Yield: 8 servings · **Dietary Notes:** Alcoholic, Vegetarian

Equipment: Medium saucepan, mesh strainer, pitcher

Cumin Ginger Tea

6 cups water

2 tablespoons (10 g) pink peppercorn

1 tablespoon (9 g) cumin seeds

4-inch (10-cm) piece ginger, sliced and peeled

5 dried loquats

1 orange

2 limes

¼ cup (60g) sugar

2 tablespoons honey

Crimson Cider (Ala Mhigan Variety) per serving

¼ cup (60 ml) cumin ginger tea

½ ounce (15 ml) bourbon

½ ounce (15 ml) raspberry liquor

Juice of ½ lime

⅓ cup (80 ml) club soda

Crimson Cider (Doman Variety) per serving

¼ cup (60 ml) cumin ginger tea

½ ounce (15 ml) sake

½ ounce (15 ml) Midori

Juice of ½ lemon

⅓ cup (80 ml) club soda

For the cumin ginger tea

1. In a saucepan over medium-high heat, combine all of the tea ingredients and bring to a boil. Reduce the heat and simmer for 25 minutes. Strain into a pitcher and allow to cool completely. Place in the refrigerator and let chill overnight. The tea can be served without alcohol as is.

For the crimson cider (Ala Mhigan variety)

1. Fill a cocktail shaker with ice and add the cumin ginger tea, bourbon, raspberry liquor, and lime juice and shake vigorously. Strain into a lowball glass and add club soda.

For the crimson cider (Doman variety)

1. Fill a cocktail shaker with ice and add the cumin ginger tea, sake, Midori, and lemon juice. Shake vigorously. Strain into a lowball glass and add club soda.

DOMAN TEA

Okay, okay, look.
*This tea here is the best, yes, yes, it is! It's got tasty persimmons, some good ginger, but the green tea is just the **BEST**. Very refreshing, very good, very Gyohan! I love drinking this tea—it's great. Did I mention the permissions? Oh, I mean **persimmons**. Yes, yes, persimmons. And the green tea, don't forget that!*

> Ask Gyohan to write the introduction **before** he drinks tea next time. There's no alcohol, but Namazu don't handle their tea well.

Difficulty: Easy · **Prep Time:** 15 minutes · **Cook Time:** 30 minutes
Yield: 4 servings · **Dietary Notes:** Vegan

Equipment: Medium saucepan, mesh strainer, pitcher

2-inch piece (5-cm) ginger, peeled and sliced

1 cinnamon stick

2 dried persimmons, sliced, plus slices for garnish (optional)

¼ cup (50 g) beet sugar

4 cups (1 L) water

2 tablespoons loose-leaf green tea

1. In a saucepan over medium-high heat, combine the ginger, cinnamon stick, dried persimmons, sugar, and water and bring to a boil. Reduce the heat and simmer for 20 minutes.

2. Add the tea leaves and simmer for another 2 minutes. Strain into a pitcher and let cool completely. Place in the refrigerator to chill overnight. The tea can be served with slices of persimmons as a garnish if you like.

ESPRESSO CON PANNA

I heard all about the Warrior of Light visiting Matoya's Cave, so I wanted to sneak in and take a peek for myself. I had no idea I would run into one of my favorite Scions, Y'shtola, relaxing with a book and a hot beverage. I wanted to sneak up and get a closer look, but as I approached, Y'shtola looked right at me! I've never been spotted before while sneaking, kupo. I panicked and asked her what she was drinking; she chuckled and offered me some espresso, then went back to her studies.

Difficulty: Easy · **Prep Time:** 15 minutes
Yield: 1 serving · **Dietary Notes:** Vegetarian

Equipment: Medium bowl, whisk

Whipped Cream

2 tablespoons heavy cream

2 tablespoons sour cream

1 tablespoon powdered sugar

¼ teaspoon vanilla extract

2 shots of espresso

1. In a bowl, combine the ingredients for the whipped cream and whisk until the mixture forms stiff peaks.

2. Pour the espresso shots in a cup and top with the whipped cream.

HI-ELIXIR

*I got lost in Ul'dah and wandered into the Alchemists' Guild. It wasn't the cooking I had in mind, no, no, but all the cauldrons and beakers got me curious, so I watched as they mixed potions and draughts. I started reading the whiteboards with complex recipes when I had a moment of Namazu inspiration for a drink of my own! It won't heal you quite the same way, but it's very tasty, very refreshing.*

Difficulty: Easy · **Prep Time:** 15 minutes
Yield: 1 serving · **Dietary Notes:** Alcoholic, Vegan

Equipment: Cocktail shaker, muddler, fine-mesh strainer

½ rosemary sprig
Ice
1 ounce (30 ml) curacao
1 ounce (30 ml) gin
1 ounce (30 ml) triple sec
2 ounces (60 ml) lime juice
½ ounce (15 ml) maple syrup

1. In a cocktail shaker, muddle the rosemary sprig. Fill the shaker with ice and add the remaining ingredients. Shake vigorously. Pour through a fine-mesh strainer into glass.

HOT CHOCOLATE

Mogria and I were walking through Ishgard when she spotted a silver-haired Elezen with a long spear and became very excited. I didn't catch his name, no, no, but he saw Mogria's boundless joy and invited us for fancy hot chocolate drinks. I was enjoying my glass when I noticed the large salt rock in the middle of the tavern table and had a sudden flash of inspiration. Very sweet, very salty! But the Elezen stopped my fin and suggested I find salt to complement the drink elsewhere.

Difficulty: Easy · **Prep Time:** 15 minutes · **Cook Time:** 15 minutes
Yield: 2 serving · **Dietary Notes:** Vegetarian

Equipment: Medium saucepan, whisk

2 cups (500 ml) oat milk

½ cup (118 ml) heavy cream

2 tablespoons sugar

¼ cup (60 ml) maple syrup

½ teaspoon ground cardamom

Pinch of salt

2 tablespoons cocoa powder

1 ounce (30 g) dark chocolate, chopped

Whipped cream (optional)

1. In a medium saucepan over medium heat, combine the milk, heavy cream, sugar, maple syrup, ground cardamon, salt, and cocoa powder. Bring to a low boil, then add the chopped chocolate. Cook, stirring occasionally, until the chocolate is melted.

2. Divide between 2 cups. Serve with a dollop of whipped cream (if using).

ISHGARDIAN TEA

When we started our travels, I took Gyohan to Ishgard to prepare. I wasn't expecting the cold to be so rough on him, but he was frozen solid by the time we arrived at the Forgotten Knight. I asked for some Ishgardian tea, one of my favorites, kupo. It turns out Namazu don't handle their tea well, and Gyohan was slurring his kupos and couldn't waddle straight. Ugh, but he won't stop talking about how good the tea was, so I had to find him this recipe.

Difficulty: Easy · **Prep Time:** 5 minutes · **Cook Time:** 15 minutes
Yield: 2 servings · **Dietary Notes:** Vegan

Equipment: Medium saucepan, whisk, fine-mesh sieve, kitchen thermometer

1 cup (250 ml) oat milk

½ cup (125 ml) almond milk

1 tablespoon maple syrup

¼ teaspoon ground cardamom

¼ teaspoon ground cinnamon

1 tablespoon loose-leaf white tea

1 tablespoon loose-leaf green tea (sencha)

1 tablespoon loose-leaf black tea

2 tablespoons hot water

1. In a medium saucepan over medium-high heat, combine the oat milk, almond milk, maple syrup, cardamom, and cinnamon. Whisk the ingredients together and heat until the mixture registers 200°F (95°C).

2. In a bowl or small pan, combine the white, green, and black tea leaves and the hot water. Let steep for 30 seconds. Add the milk mixture and let steep for 2 minutes. Strain through a fine-mesh sieve into 2 cups and serve.

LEMONADE

My moogle friends in the Twelveswood told me about a super-sweet lemon drink made with the honey from Fullflower Comb in the East Shroud, but they are all too nervous to ask for a glass, kupo. I asked why they would ask for a glass when they have two perfectly good hands for taking, but they didn't understand, and now I don't understand them! Family can be so weird sometimes, kupo, but this drink is delicious!

Difficulty: Easy · **Prep Time:** 15 minutes · **Cook Time:** 10 minutes
Yield: 4 servings · **Dietary Notes:** Vegetarian

Equipment: Medium saucepan, whisk, large pitcher

Simple Honey Syrup
½ cup (100 g) sugar
½ cup (185 g) honey
1 cup (240 ml) water

Lemonade
Simple honey syrup
1 cup (250 ml) fresh lemon juice
3 cups (750 ml) water

1. In a medium saucepan over medium-high heat, combine the sugar, honey, and water and bring to a simmer, stirring occasionally. Once the sugar and honey dissolve, remove from the heat to cool.

2. In a large pitcher, stir the simple honey syrup and lemon juice together. Add the water. If the flavor is too strong, add an additional cup of water. Place in the refrigerator overnight to chill before serving.

MATCHA

I have often found Tataru drinking matcha in the Umineko Teahouse in Kugane while talking to all sorts of people. Sometimes they look very well-to-do, and other times they look a bit suspect, kupo! I love watching how Tataru makes the matcha and drinks it the proper Hingashi way; she looks so sophisticated! I had to take notes, for I am also going to be sophisticated one day.

Difficulty: Easy · **Prep Time:** 10 minutes · **Cook Time:** 15 minutes
Yield: 2 servings · **Dietary Notes:** Vegan

Equipment: Medium saucepan, whisk, fine-mesh strainer, bamboo whisk, kitchen thermometer

¾ cup (180 ml) oat milk

1 tablespoon (20 g) honey

Pinch of salt

2 teaspoons matcha powder

½ cup (125 ml) hot water (175°F/79°C)

1. In a medium saucepan over medium-high heat, whisk together the oat milk, honey, and salt. Heat the mixture until it registers 175°F (80°C).

2. Sift the matcha into a bowl. Add the hot water and whisk the matcha until completely smooth. Combine the sweetened oat milk and matcha in a cup.

MULLED TEA

This is a tasty drink I found at the Quicksand in Ul'dah. It seemed like everyone was drinking it, but I wouldn't let Gyohan drink it and make a fool of himself, kupo, so I described what it tasted like. I've had tea before, but this had far more spices and herbs than I'm used to. I need to bring this back to Moghome—I bet other moogles would love it too!

Difficulty: Easy · **Prep Time:** 15 minutes · **Cook Time:** 30 minutes
Yield: 2 servings · **Dietary Notes:** Vegetarian

Equipment: Medium saucepan, mesh strainer

2 cinnamon sticks
2-inch (5-cm) piece ginger, sliced
3 whole cloves
3 cups (750 ml) water
2 tablespoons Assam tea leaves
2 tablespoons honey

1. In a medium saucepan over medium-high heat, combine the cinnamon, ginger, cloves, and water. Bring to a boil, then reduce the heat and simmer for 20 minutes.

2. Add the tea leaves and honey and simmer for another 2 minutes. Strain and divide between 2 cups.

PIXIEBERRY TEA

I was daydreaming by the Rising Stones when a weird creature I've never seen before fluttered right next to me. They said their name was Feo Ul, and they thought I'd be available to deliver something, but I explained that I was far too busy waiting for the Warrior of Light to show up, kupo. Their eyes lit up and they exclaimed "Oh, my sapling is nearby? How lovely, maybe I'll wait as well!" and they magicked up a drink I've never seen before. Feo Ul said it was one of their favorites, a pixieberry tea as they described it, and offered me a glass.

Difficulty: Medium · **Prep Time:** 30 minutes · **Rest Time:** 12 hours · **Cook Time:** 30 minutes
Yield: 8 to 10 servings · **Dietary Notes:** Vegan

Equipment: Medium saucepan, airtight container, whisk

Strawberry Syrup

1 cup (250 ml) water
½ cup (100 g) granulated sugar
½ cup (118 g) beet sugar
1 pound (500 g) strawberries
Small handful of mint leaves

Per Serving

3 to 4 strawberry slices
½ cup (125 ml) cold green tea
5 tablespoons (80 ml) strawberry syrup
½ cup (125 ml) carbonated water
Mint leaves

1. In a medium saucepan over medium-high heat, combine the water, granulated sugar, and beet sugar. Whisk until the sugar has dissolved. Add the strawberries and bring to a boil. Reduce the heat and simmer for 12 minutes.

2. Remove the pan from the heat and add the mint leaves. Let sit for 10 minutes. Strain the syrup into an airtight container. Once cooled, the syrup can be stored in the refrigerator for at least 12 hours and up to 2 weeks.

3. Place the strawberry slices in a tall glass. Add the strawberry syrup and green tea to the glass and stir together. Add the carbonated water and lightly swirl with a spoon. Garnish with fresh mint.

WARMWINE

I ran into the Warrior of Light's friend, Thancred, resting at the hot springs in Camp Bronze Lake. He looked worn down and tired, so I looked around and found a bottle of Warmwine that someone wasn't using and brought it to him. He was surprised to see me, but he appreciated the gesture and smiled. After I left, I saw his smile disappear again. Hopefully the hot springs and the hot drink help ease whatever ails him.

Difficulty: Easy · **Prep Time:** 15 minutes · **Cook Time:** 15 minutes
Yield: 2 servings · **Dietary Notes:** Alcoholic, Vegetarian

Equipment: Large pot

1 orange, sliced

⅓ pound (150 g) cherries, pitted

6 whole cloves

1 cinnamon stick

2 star anise

1 (750 ml) bottle dry red wine

1½ cups (375 ml) tart cherry juice

⅔ cup (215 g) honey

1. In a large pot over medium heat, combine all of the ingredients. Bring to a low simmer, and simmer for 15 minutes. Serve hot.

X-POTION

 Mogria took me to an apparently important building in Vesper Bay called the Waking Sands. She was so excited, but we were both surprised to find one of the Scions there, looking through big dusty books and reading fortunes. I asked him about the different drinks on the table, yes, yes, but he was so hard to understand that I couldn't catch any of it. I fell asleep and hit my head on the hard floor, so the nice man offered me a potion for my bump. It was pretty tasty!

> I can't believe Gyohan embarrassed me in front of Urianger, kupo! Now I can never return there.

Difficulty: Easy · **Prep Time:** 15 minutes · **Cook Time:** 30 minutes
Yield: 6 servings · **Dietary Notes:** Alcoholic, Vegetarian

Equipment: Medium saucepan, whisk, large pitcher

Simple Lavender Syrup

½ cup (100 g) sugar
¼ cup (85 g) honey
1 cup (250 ml) water
3 tablespoons dried lavender

Lavender Citrus Juice

½ cup (125 ml) lemon juice
½ cup (125 ml) lime juice
Simple lavender syrup
1 cup (250 ml) water
1 drop purple food dye, optional

Per X-Potion

1 ounce (30 ml) gin
2 ounces (60 ml) Moscato
4 ounces (125 ml) Lavender Citrus Juice

1. In a saucepan over medium-high heat, stir together the sugar, honey, and water. Once the sugar and honey dissolve, add the dried lavender and bring to a simmer. Reduce the heat to medium-low and simmer for 25 minutes. Remove from the heat and let cool.

2. In a large pitcher, mix all the ingredients for lavender citrus juice together. Place in the refrigerator overnight to chill before serving.

3. Combine all the ingredients in a tall glass. Lightly stir together and serve.

> *If you don't feel like adding alcohol to this, you can enjoy the lavender citrus juice on its own.*

DIETARY CONSIDERATIONS

 During our travels, we learned that many individuals have specific limitations to what they can eat. It is important to make adjustments and substitutions, so everyone is able to enjoy the feast. Namazu, for example, don't handle tea very well, kupo! And other moogles don't like eating things that aren't kupo nuts. They aren't refined like me.

ADAPTING TO VEGETARIAN DIETS

Several recipes in this book are vegetarian or vegan friendly. Many recipes can be adapted to your dietary needs. Replace meat broths/stocks with vegetable broths/stocks. Swap out proteins with your favorite grilled vegetables or meat substitutes. This will affect the cooking times, so plan ahead.

ADAPTING TO GLUTEN-FREE DIETS

For most recipes, you can use equal ratios of gluten substitute for flour, but be prepared to modify the quantity just in case the consistency seems off compared to how it is described in the recipes.

ADAPTING TO LACTOSE-FREE DIETS

Feel free to replace milk and heavy cream with your favorite dairy-free milk. There are also plenty of alternatives to replace butter in recipes. Replacing butter with oil isn't usually recommended, because it doesn't give the same consistency needed for certain recipes. If you do use oil instead, introduce it in smaller amounts.

Recipe	Vegetarian	Vegan	Gluten Free
Breakfast			
Almond Cream Croissants	V		
The Minstrel's Ballad: Almond Cream Croissants	V		
Dodo Omelette	V		
Farmer's Breakfast			GF
La Noscean Toast	V		
Lemon Waffle	V		
Nutrient-rich Porridge	V		GF
Oriental Breakfast			
Royal Eggs			
Salmon Muffins			
Wildwood Scrambled Eggs	V		GF
Appetizers			
Crab Crouquette			
Deviled Eggs			GF
Forest Miq'abob	V	V+	GF
Futo-maki Roll			
Jerked Jhammel			
Meat Miq'abob			
Popoto Salad	V		GF
Sandwich Basket			
Steppe Salad	GF		
Tuna Miq'abob			
Breads			
Bacon Bread			
Cornbread	V		
Honey Muffin	V		
Ishgardian Muffin	V		
Knight's Bread	V		
Walnut Bread	V		
Soups and Stews			
Bouillabaisse			GF
Cawl Cennin			GF
Exquisite Beef Stew			
Lentils and Chestnuts	V	V+	GF
Miso Soup with Tofu			GF
Oden			
Orobon Stew			
Skybuilders' Stew			
Main Dishes			
Banh Xeo			GF
Battered Fish			
Boscaiola			

Recipe	Vegetarian	Vegan	Gluten Free
Creamy Salmon Pasta			
Deep-fried Okeanis			
Mole Loaf			
Pan-fried Mahi-Mahi			
Pizza	V		
Pork Kakuni			
Rare Roast Beef			
Starlight Dodo			GF
Stuffed Cabbage Rolls			GF
Trapper's Quiche			
Sides			
Chawan-mushi			
Cheese Risotto			GF
Imam Bayildi	V	V+	GF
Mashed Popotoes	V		GF
Mushroom Sauté	V		GF
Popotoes au Gratin	V		
Ratatouille	V	V+	GF
Spinach Sauté	V		
Desserts			
Apple Strudel	V		
Cheese Soufflé	V		
Chocobo Cake	V		
Coffee Biscuit	V		
Dango	V	V+	GF
Kupo Nuts	V		GF
Papanasi	V		
Princess Pudding	V		
Rolanberry Cheesecake	V		
Sesame Cookies	V		
Drinks			
Crimson Cider	V		GF
Doman Tea	V	V+	GF
Espresso con Panna	V		GF
Hi-Elixir	V	V+	GF
Hot Chocolate	V		GF
Ishgardian Tea	V	V+	GF
Lemonade	V		GF
Matcha	V	V+	GF
Mulled Tea	V		GF
Pixieberry Tea	V	V+	GF
Warmwine	V		GF
X-Potion	V		GF

ABOUT THE AUTHOR

Victoria Rosenthal launched her blog, Pixelated Provisions, in 2012 to combine her lifelong passions for video games and food by recreating consumables found in many of her favorite games. When she isn't experimenting in the kitchen and dreaming up new recipes, she spends her days developing graphics for NASA. She resides in Houston, Texas, with her husband and corgi. Victoria is also the author of *Fallout: The Vault Dweller's Official Cookbook*, *Destiny: The Official Cookbook*, and *Street Fighter: The Official Street Food Cookbook*.

ACKNOWLEDGMENTS

Thanks Jeff Rosenthal, Kanji, Nick Esparza, Kevin Giesler, and Kate McKean for joining me on this Trial Roulette. Thanks to Rene Rodriguez, Matt Thomas, Kevin Stich, Irvin Chavira, Harry Readinger, Nina Freeman, Elaine Gray, Will Baker, Forrest Porter, Saam Pahlavan, Brock Wright, my family, and the Pixelated Provisions' community for all the support to complete this Wondrous Tails.

SPECIAL THANKS TO THE TEAM AT SQUARE ENIX

Amanda Asato	Lisa Kawashima	Annika Schumann
Flanna Borgeson-Leake	Minami Kobayashi	Saori Spencer-Hill
Natasha Cheng	Mizuho Kondo	Janet Swallow
Linda Fuhlendorf	Nils Kröger	Juno Tang
Christopher Galvan	Keiko Mishima	Cameron Turner
Latysha Hadidjaja	Haider Abass Raza Muttaqi	Simon Wells
Eri Hamada	Adam Pelc	Benjamin Wilford
Matt Hilton	Clément Ruggeri	FINAL FANTASY XIV Development and Operations teams
Luke Karmali	Ichitaro Saito	

INSIGHT
EDITIONS

PO Box 3088
San Rafael, CA 94912
www.insighteditions.com

Find us on Facebook: www.facebook.com/InsightEditions

Follow us on Twitter: @insighteditions

Library of Congress Cataloging-in-Publication Data available.

ISBN: 978-1-64722-511-7
ISBN (GAMESTOP): 978-1-64722-641-1

Please note that the recipes presented in this cookbook are interpretations of items found within
FINAL FANTASY XIV and may not appear identical to those found in-game.

Publisher: Raoul Goff
VP of Licensing and Partnerships: Vanessa Lopez
VP of Creative: Chrissy Kwasnik
VP of Manufacturing: Alix Nicholaeff
Editorial Director: Vicki Jaeger
Designer: Monique Narboneta
Senior Editor: Jennifer Sims
Associate Editor: Maya Alpert
Senior Production Editor: Jennifer Bentham
Production Manager: Greg Steffen
Senior Production Manager, Subsidiary Rights: Lina s Palma

ROOTS of PEACE   REPLANTED PAPER

Insight Editions, in association with Roots of Peace, will plant two trees for each tree used in the manufacturing
of this book. Roots of Peace is an internationally renowned humanitarian organization dedicated to eradicating
land mines worldwide and converting war-torn lands into productive farms and wildlife habitats. Roots of Peace
will plant two million fruit and nut trees in Afghanistan and provide farmers there with the skills and support
necessary for sustainable land use.

Manufactured in Turkey by Insight Editions

10 9 8 7 6 5 4 3 2